THE
GOD WHO
HEARS

W. Bingham Hunter

INTERVARSITY PRESS
DOWNERS GROVE, ILLINOIS 60515

InterVarsity Press is the book-publishing division of Inter-Varsity Christian Fellowship, a student movement active on campus at hundreds of universities, colleges and schools of nursing. For information about local and regional activities, write IVCF, 233 Langdon St., Madison, WI 53703.

Cover illustration: Greg Wray

ISBN 0-87784-604-9

Printed in the United States of America

Library of Congress Cataloging in Publication Data
Hunter, W. Bingham, 1943-
  The God who hears.

Bibliography: p.
  Includes index.
  1. Prayer.   2. Providence and government of God.
I. Title.
BV220.H86   1986   248.3'2   86-7268
ISBN 0-87784-604-9 (pbk.)

28 27 26 25 24 23 22 21 20 19 18 17 16 15
15 14 13 12 11 10 09 08 07 06 05 04 03 02

For Jo-Ann, Doug and Hillery

Acknowledgments

Production of this volume has spanned several years and was encouraged by many friends and colleagues. My initial studies of prayer were undertaken in facilities provided by the Faculty of Divinity, Aberdeen University, Scotland. Development of several important chapters was aided by a Faculty Research Grant provided by BIOLA University, Inc. The book was completed during a sabbatical leave granted to me by Talbot School of Theology in facilities kindly made available by the Faculty of Divinity, Cambridge University, England.

1
Who Does God Hear?

I don't know who God hears," said my anguished friend, "but it certainly isn't me."

One of the world's greatest religious historians Friedrich Heiler once said that prayer is "the hearthstone of all piety."[1] This thought would seem to be safely ensconced in the shrine of theological truth, but I wonder if it accurately reflects how most people feel about prayer.

Many of the honest but not so eminent Christians I know have felt (at *least* once) that prayer was more of a stumblingblock than a hearthstone in their spiritual lives. In 1968 *Newsweek* ran a feature entitled "Can Modern Man Pray?" It concluded that most could not.[2] More recent surveys show that although an astoundingly

large number of Americans claim to have religion, the clergy report
that prayer and prayer groups are "especially successful" in only one
per cent of their churches.[3] *Los Angeles Times* staff writer Dick Rora-
back neatly summed up the mood of our age:

> The computer people are fond of telling us that this is the Age
> of Communication.
>
> Sure.
>
> Children can't communicate with parents, parents can't com-
> municate with *their* parents, and hardly anybody, it seems, can
> get through to God, even after 6 p.m.[4]

To me all this is sobering, but none of it is surprising. Believers
from across the spectrum of maturity and denominational prefer-
ence tell me that God no longer seems to care whether they pray
or not. Others freely (if sometimes tearfully) confess that they can
no longer ask him anything. They cannot take the personal devas-
tation which results when something absolutely vital to them is
completely ignored by God. Like my friend, they don't think God
hears them at all.

I think we got into this state for several reasons. First, prayer was
never a heresy in the early church, and so no council sat to define
and clarify what orthodoxy in personal spirituality means. As a
result we have all been doing what seems right in our own eyes.
Even today, many systematic theology texts omit prayer, and those
which include it can't agree on where it goes: a means of grace? an
implication of the atonement? the work of the Spirit? Most evangelical seminaries do not have a course on prayer, and those which
do invariably make it an elective—something apparently not essential to the practice of ministry. Congregations have eventually, and
inevitably, got the message.

Second, modern science and technology have left little space in
twentieth-century life for ancient supernatural religion. Philos-
ophers and theologians have told us God is dead—or at least "in
process" somewhere—while sociologists catalog the results of the
"secularization" of the church. Most of us are just too busy to
wonder much about why prayer seems irrelevant. But of course it

wouldn't matter: God has become too small to intervene in the world anymore, and we are too sophisticated to ask him to anyway.

Third, teaching and preaching about prayer often distort Scripture. We are told to *use* the Lord's promises as if they had no context in biblical literature or life, and we are encouraged to claim things the Bible never names. The name of Jesus is invoked over things he wouldn't recognize. And some of our godliest folk are tortured by barbarian banter: "Maybe *someday* you'll have enough faith to be healed."

Fourth, and finally, when we pray we don't know what we're doing. Christians can find lots of texts on what prayer means and what it presumes. And its importance and significance, both personally and corporately, are discussed at length. But very few of our leaders and scholars seem willing to say what prayer *is.* An astounding number of Christians believe prayer is a way to get God to give you what you want. And being so convinced, they are easy prey for hawkers of techniques and equipment which seem to guarantee results. Personal communication with our Lord is thus commonly thought of in mechanical and economic terms.

Sure, I know, there *are* lots of thrilling answers to prayer. We can read about powerful petition in dozens of books and articles every

THE FAMILY CIRCUS®　　　　　　　　**By Bil Keane**

"Listen to this, God, here's an offer you can't refuse."

year and see supersupplicators almost every month on TV. But all this only increases the heartache, guilt and frustration of those who feel they can't, or are afraid to, take prayer seriously. It is hard to rejoice with those who rejoice . . . if you feel you have to cry alone. When is the last time you felt free to "share" your tremendous *unanswered* prayer? I am convinced that a huge, but largely secret, group of Christians genuinely longs to know both God and themselves better and are weary of having to sing "It is well with my soul" with their fingers crossed. I write for them.

This book is an attempt to be *honest* about the existence of serious prayer difficulties, *encouraging* to those who hope for reality in their relationship with our Lord, and *faithful* to Holy Scripture. You should know before you go further that I passionately disagree with the notion that prayer is a way to get from God what we want. Christian prayer, as explained in Scripture, seems something else entirely: *Prayer is a means God uses to give us what he wants.*

The most important word in this definition is *God*. I say this because at root most of our prayer difficulties are theological problems. "Theological" in the sense that we simply do not focus enough on the *Theos* (the Greek word for God). So the following chapters discuss prayer in light of what the Bible says about God. Prayer really makes sense only against the background of God's nature and attributes. First, we must know whom we are talking to. Second, we have got to know ourselves. Third, we need someone who understands *both* God and ourselves to show us how to do it. The organization of the book reflects these realities.

Part 1 (chapters 2-7) examines the nature and attributes of God from the standpoint of *why* the Bible says what it does about prayer. It is because God is holy, that we are asked to confess; it is because he knows everything, that we must be honest. Because he is sovereign, we must ask according to his will, and so on. Part 2 (chapters 8-13) explores the implications of being God's children: for example, we praise him because he made us; we love and forgive because we want to be like him. Part 3 (chapters 14-15) concludes the study by looking at the One who was not ashamed to call us his brothers and sisters. Christ is the embodiment of what it means to know God and call on him as his child. He is our example, and we must learn to pray as he did.

My object in writing is to help people like you begin thinking more biblically about God and to help you understand *why* he wants to have you talk with him. A second goal is to encourage you to share your prayer experience with others; so I have placed discussion questions at the end of each chapter. You are not alone in what you think about things like unanswered prayer and having enough faith.

This is obviously not the only book on Christian prayer;[5] there are dozens of volumes on the topic. But I think this may be the only study organized so as to discuss prayer in the context of the whole Christian life—as an aspect of living as God's child and an obedient disciple of Christ. From a biblical point of view, prayer is related to everything that we are and everything that God is. God does *not* respond to our prayers. God responds to *us:* to our whole life. What we say to him cannot be separated from what we think, feel, will and do. Prayer is communication from whole persons to the Wholeness which is the living God. Prayer is misunderstood until we see it this way.

There *are* answers to many of our "prayer questions," but to approach answering them we must start to think more biblically about God *and* ourselves. "Authentic, biblical, evangelical prayer," as Donald Bloesch says, "is now in eclipse. . . . The disciplines of devotion have receded into the background as people seek instant salvation through prescribed and easily learned techniques."[6] Yet learning to think biblically about God, ourselves and prayer is worth the effort. Delighting in God is *the* way to greatness—no matter where your personal aspirations lie.[7] The chapters which follow are intended to help you grow, expand and develop richness in your relationship with our Lord. Our heavenly Father himself is our greatest treasure. Praying more effectively is largely a matter of learning to know *him* as the desire of our hearts. That's where we'll begin.

Questions for Thought and Discussion

1. Why is it so hard to be honest with others about our struggles with prayer?

2. What can be done to create an atmosphere among Christians in which such feelings could be discussed openly?

3. C. S. Lewis once said, "That gnat-like cloud of petty anxieties and decisions about the conduct of the next hour have interfered with my prayers more often than any passion or appetite whatever."[8] What do you think interferes with your prayers? Make a list. Do men and women have different kinds of difficulties?

4. How is the Christian understanding of spirituality different from when your parents were your age? How is it the same?

5. What is your initial impression about the approach taken toward prayer in chapter one?

6. What sort of books on spirituality do you like? Why?

7. What do you hope to get from this book? Why are you reading it?

Part 1
What Is God Like?

2
Holy:
How Can I Approach
Him?

Suddenly the screen went stark white. And it stayed white for five or six seconds. It was 1970 and I was watching a film, but my thoughts flashed back to the original event, captured by ultra-high speed cameras protected by concrete bunkers and leaded glass. Only milliseconds before, there had been ships in a lagoon formed by a coral atoll called Bikini. Now there was only blinding light. Some of the ships, part of the sea and one of the little islands were completely vaporized in a flash of awesome whiteness.

The film was taken in 1954 when the first hydrogen fusion weapon (an H-bomb) was tested in the South Pacific. You are probably wondering, "What is an image like this doing in a book on prayer?" It is here because the whiteness of that screen remains, for me, the most powerful illustration of the way biblical writers express God's holiness:

God is light; in him there is no darkness at all. (1 Jn 1:5)

God, the blessed and only Ruler, the King of kings and Lord of lords, who alone is immortal and who lives in unapproachable light, whom no one has seen or can see . . . (1 Tim 6:15-16)

Our God is a consuming fire. (Heb 12:29)

God's moral purity—his inherent personal righteousness and holiness—is symbolized in Scripture as light: blinding, unending, undiminishing, dazzling whiteness. Even the newest believer has read in John 1:5 that with the coming of the Lord Jesus, the light of God was made to shine in the darkness on this island in space called the world. But few of us consider the implications of God's light for human holiness. As John 1:5 goes on to say, "the darkness has not understood it." Comprehending holiness is difficult. And it is life changing. So Christians have developed ways of keeping the idea at a comfortable distance.

The Holy Wimp

We have a general tendency to think of *holiness* as the absence of moral darkness or evil, such as wrongdoing and sin. Told that the idea behind biblical holiness comes from words meaning "to be separate," we readily envision the holy fellow as one who is separate from wrong and hence "doesn't smoke, dance, drink or chew or go with girls who sniff glue." And because behavioral standards in the Christian community are couched in terms like "no," "don't" and "avoid," a *negative* notion about holiness becomes second nature. We understand instantly, as every cartoonist well knows, that the rather thin (probably prudish, but always very proper) wimp in the black suit is the embodiment of that bland existence which passes among us as moral purity.

And what of the "God" who selected him? The God who delights in this sort of fellow is an ancient withered celestial prune. Testy and touchy to the uttermost, he scans the world, ever hopeful of spotting a creature at whom he can screech, "You, you there with

Forrest Piesko in Good Housekeeping

your hand in the cookie jar . . . You look like you're thinking about having fun. Cut it out. Right now. And don't you think about it again. EVER!"

Seeing a travelog on India and hearing that the fakir on the bed of nails is "a *very* holy man" . . . well, it all hangs together. Holiness is supposed to hurt; and it makes you different and unattractive.

In such a context, "Be holy, because I am holy" (1 Pet 1:16) hardly seems like good news. Holiness is a burden of negativism which lives down to our worst suspicions: "don't, Don't, DON'T!" So naturally, we don't.

Why Not?
But why is unholiness so easy? And why do hymns like "Take Time to Be Holy" seem to make so little sense? (Does it take time *not* to do something?)

A major factor is certainly *our willingness to accept an unbalanced, overly negative understanding of holiness*. Far from a separation from the world, holiness is a *separation to positive goodness*, with separation from wrong as its consequence. God is *not* a crotchety, self-righteous prude who delights in never doing anything wrong. He is a living, dynamic Being actively involved in *making wrong right*. He is scintillating light. Holiness is a positive concept and means a life engaged in helping people who hurt. Satan feels little threat from a thousand pious pretenders, but someone like Mother Teresa of Calcutta must be profoundly disturbing. The demons understand God's holiness— and shudder (Jas 2:19). Only the children of light find it easy to shrug and walk away.

Another reason why holiness is so hard to understand is that *Christians are like fish, living in a fluid medium (society) which has become so morally murky* that "light" seems abnormal. We were born in dirty water and have gotten used to it. Mud and murk are normal; clean and light are threatening. We can see rotten things on the bottom, but assume we cannot get stuck in the muck if we keep moving. And besides, we generally swim (in circles) higher up in the pond. We have learned to live comfortably with unholiness and see lots of others wearing *Ichthus* pins who do too.[1]

A final factor, which is even more important, is *our general loss of holy terror*. Christian appreciation for God's astounding gift of love, forgiveness and reconciliation in Christ has been allowed to consume the awesome reality of his terrible holiness. God has become our "buddy." It seems foreign to speak about God as Isaiah did: "Go into the rocks, hide in the ground from dread of the Lord and the splendor of his majesty" (Is 2:10).

We have turned statements about unhindered freedom to speak openly during prayer (what the New Testament calls "confidence") into license for flippancy, and we have made remarks about the privilege of access to God through Christ (what the New Testament calls "boldness") into sanctions for arrogance. Somehow we have forgotten that Jesus, who taught us to call God *Abba* (Dear Father), also called him *Holy* Father, *Righteous* Father and *Lord* of heaven and earth, when he prayed. (See Mk 14:36; Jn 17:11; and Lk 10:21).

The Reality of Fear
Since irrational fears ("phobias") have destructive effects on human lives, it is hard to see fearing God as a good thing. But many of the arguments against holy terror are based on faulty theological systems ("the 'fearful' image of God belongs to the dispensation of Law"), imprecise exegesis ("God has not given us a spirit of fear"), or the existence of psychopathology ("some Christians do have phobias about God"). I assert that without a sense of God's awesome holiness, and the consequent "fear," we simply do not have biblical religion, either positively—"The fear of the LORD is the beginning of wisdom" (Ps 111:10)—or negatively—"Concerning the sinfulness of the wicked: There is no fear of God before his eyes" (Ps 36:1).

The dynamics of fearing God are helpfully explained by Robert Morosco:

> One's ultimate fear-object is that which he reveres above all else in life. . . . This is the position which legitimately belongs only to the creature's Creator, though this is often not the case. One's supreme fear-object warrants total regard and esteem. . . .
>
> Hence the biblical translation "revere" or "respect" or "regard" is actually close to what the writers of Scripture had in mind [when they spoke of the "fear of the Lord"]. . . . Theological fear is not primarily dread or repulsion for the fear-object, but surrender to [God's] authority.[2]

Fearing God is thus not irrational. It is the only course open to a thinking Christian. In fact, not fearing God is irrational. It forces us to deny the reality of God's holiness, power and presence. So Morosco is right when he says:

> Only by fearing Jehovah is reality ultimately viewed as it truly is. In order to replace God with another supreme fear-object [fear of failure, or fear of other people, for example], reality has

to be distorted (i.e., the character of the living God must be altered).[3]

Those who do not fear God in the biblical sense either do not understand, or find themselves forced to deny, the facts of existence. And such a venture into fantasy advances against truth on two fronts. It denies the fact of God's infiniteness and rejects human finiteness. No one has seen more clearly than Harry Blamires that this latter (and very common) deception is at the root of human unholiness:

> What is common to those who lack any interest in religion is failure to recognize the finitude of the finite, and especially failure to accept man's own finite status for what it is. This failure is the source alike of moral evil and of intellectual confusion. All forms of moral evil have their roots in a tacit denial of human finitude—of the contingent and wholly dependent nature of man's existence. . . .
>
> Man behaves as though he were not a dependent creature with a limited and temporary existence in a limited and temporal universe. Covetousness and greed for power both express defiance of finitude. Covetousness implies that the pursuit of earthly possessions is of ultimate significance: it implies that to possess within the finite is a state of fulfillment. This is nonsensical. There is no stability or security in possession within the finite order, where at any moment accident or death may strip or destroy. The pursuit of power implies that temporal sway and masterdom are an ultimate satisfaction: [but] finitude precludes such satisfactions within its own domain. . . . In these pursuits, and in a thousand others, man conceals from himself the fact that finitude sets a term to all activities at the temporal level.[4]

Those who do not fear God as the transcendent, holy and infinite Creator replace his power and authority with either themselves, others or material things. "They [have] exchanged the truth of God for a lie, and worshiped and served created things rather than the Creator—who is [to be] forever praised" (Rom 1:25). Having denied the realities of both divine and human nature, it seems obvious why they may have little concern for doing God's will and are unlikely to pray according to it.

It took decades of discipline through suffering before Israel began to take "Be holy, because I am holy" (Lev 11:44) seriously enough to fear and call on the Holy One out of pure hearts. One wonders just when and how reality will dawn on us. There is certainly no way around it with respect to effective prayer: "We know that God does not hear sinners; but if anyone is God-fearing, and does His will, He hears him" (Jn 9:31 NASB).

Toward Personal Honesty
Explicit statements affirming God's holiness are found throughout Scripture. The Old Testament prophets make it especially clear that because of his own intrinsic holiness, God cannot respond positively to unholiness in his creatures:

Thine eyes are too pure to approve evil, and Thou canst not look on wickedness with favor. (Hab 1:13 NASB)

Everyone who acts unjustly is an abomination to the LORD your God. (Deut 25:16 NASB)

The LORD detests the thoughts of the wicked. (Prov 15:26)

From words like these we know that God eschews both internal evil (thoughts) and external acts of injustice and wickedness. This directly affects the prayers of unholy people:

The LORD detests the sacrifice of the wicked, but the prayer of the upright pleases him. (Prov 15:8)

If I had cherished sin in my heart, the Lord would not have listened. (Ps 66:18)

Do not be deceived: God cannot be mocked. A man reaps what he sows. The one who sows to please his sinful nature, from that nature will reap destruction. (Gal 6:7-8)

Sin is defined in the Westminster Shorter Catechism as "any want of conformity unto—or transgression of—the LAW OF GOD." We can boil it down more: sin is the failure to live congruently with God's holiness. The Bible explains deviations from such congruency using negative terms such as:

betrayal	iniquity	transgression
error	lawlessness	trespass
falling short	missing the mark	unrighteousness

But it also states emphatically that failure to do good is equally sinful in God's eyes (see Rom 3:12). Paul says the reason for sin, whether omission of goodness or commission of unrighteousness, is grounded in the fact that "there is no *fear* of God before their eyes" (Rom 3:18).

Christians are certain that such descriptions of sin apply to those who have not accepted Christ as personal savior. We read Romans 1:18—3:18 musing, "Oh, yes, Paul, they *are* like that. Sock it to 'em." But sin also continues to live in the Christian, as texts like 1 John 1:8 and 10 make clear: "If we claim to be without sin, we deceive ourselves and the truth is not in us. . . . If we claim we have not sinned, we make him out to be a liar and his word has no place in our lives." First John is *unquestionably* addressed to Christian believers: "the children of God" (3:1).

Somehow our emphasis on God's legal justification of believers—the fact that in Christ we are regarded by God as possessing his holiness (2 Cor 5:21)—has blotted out the equally important personal reality that *all* Christians continue to struggle daily with sin until they are glorified. Truth, as John says, demands that we Christians, who are "positionally" holy due to God's grace appropriated by faith in Christ, admit the daily reality of sin in our lives and stop deceiving ourselves.

Mistakes, Both Practical and Theological

There are many reasons why Christians find it easy to live with personal and corporate sin. First, we do not really understand the nature of God's holiness. Job did, and was driven to repentance: "My ears had heard of you but now my eyes have seen you. Therefore I despise myself and repent in dust and ashes" (Job 42:5-6). Falling down or feeling awestruck before God's holiness as did Isaiah (6:1-6), Ezekiel (1:25-28) and the Elders (Rev 4:8-10) is foreign to our dignified sensibilities.

Further, since somebody else died to atone for our sin (Rom 3:25; 1 Jn 2:1-2), we have little notion of how destructive sin is or how imminent judgment is. We do not really believe that judgment (perhaps we should read "discipline/chastisement") *"begins* with the family of God" (1 Pet 4:17). Israel's experience of exile took place thousands of years ago. And modern-day persecution takes place thousands of miles away. We interpret God's delay in disciplining us as evidence of unconcern about our unholiness. Yet Paul asks in Romans 2:4, "Do you show contempt for the riches of his kindness, tolerance and patience, not realizing that God's kindness leads you toward repentance?"

We also presume on God's love when we take for granted the certainty of our eventual glorification. Since nothing can separate us from God's love in Christ (Rom 8:39), we do little about personal holiness. We misunderstand repentance and contrition, which are essential to genuine confession and consequent forgiveness and cleansing. We simply don't know what it is to mourn over sin, either personally (Mt 5:4) or corporately (Ezra 10:1).

Finally, to us God's gift of daily cleansing (1 Jn 1:9; 2:1-2) has become a trite, mechanical experience. Jesus *died* on the cross for *our* sins (yours and mine). We have become blind to the blood on our hands: the blood of Jesus, which is the *only* reason why 1 John 1:9 "works": "Without the shedding of blood there is *no* forgiveness" (Heb 9:22).

I do not counsel that we not seek to be forgiven, far from it.[5] But we must never forget the astounding cost behind all God's forgiveness:

He was pierced for our transgressions,
    he was crushed for our iniquities;
the punishment that brought us peace was upon him,
    and by his wounds we are healed. . . .
The LORD has laid on him the iniquity of us all. (Is 53:5-6)

The more we reflect on what Christ suffered to make it possible for us to be holy, the more we ought to find personal unholiness

abhorrent. John Owen put it this way:
> Bring thy lust to the Gospel—not for relief, but for further con-
> viction of its guilt; look on Him whom thou hast pierced, and be
> in bitterness. Say to thy soul, "What have I done? What love,
> what mercy, what blood, what grace have I despised and
> trampled on! Is this the return I make to the Father for His love,
> to the Son for His blood, to the Holy Spirit for His grace?"[6]

There is no more urgent basis for individual Christian holiness.
Simply put, sin hurts and grieves God, who loves us and died for
us.

We must—if we are at all rational—respond with all our being in
loving obedience to the One who "bought us" at such a horrendous
price. For me to take personal holiness lightly is to spit in the face
of Christ . . . as he hangs on the cross in agony dying to atone for
my sin.

It is little wonder sin grieves the Holy Spirit who lives in us (Eph
5:30). Yet the greater and more astounding wonder is that sin
grieves us so little. May God help us to see unholiness for what it
is (give us "salve to put on [our] eyes, so that [we] can see," Rev
3:18) and to see that sin makes us "pitiful, poor, blind and naked"
(Rev 3:17).

Raising Holiness Consciousness

Though later in this chapter I make some suggestions, I see no
"quick fix" for this state of affairs. But I am convinced that Christians who desire to pray more effectively *must* first spend more time
reading those portions of God's Word which emphasize his holiness.
Particularly neglected are the Old Testament prophets—Isaiah, Jeremiah and Ezekiel—and the Psalms.

Further, we must make the petitions of the psalms our petitions:

> Test me, O LORD, and try me,
> Examine my heart and my mind. (26:2)

> Search me, O God, and know my heart;

test me and know my anxious thoughts.
See if there is any offensive way in me. (139:24)

Finally, we must take the penitential words of David and ask the Spirit to make them ours:
Have mercy on me, O God,
according to your unfailing love;
according to your great compassion
blot out my transgressions.
Wash away all my iniquity
and cleanse me from my sin.
For I know my transgressions,
and my sin is always before me.
Against you, you only, have I sinned
and done what is evil in your sight,
so that you are proved right when you speak
and justified when you judge.
Surely I was sinful at birth,
sinful from the time my mother conceived me.
Surely you desire truth in the inner parts;
you teach me wisdom in the inmost place.
Cleanse me with hyssop,[7] and I will be clean;
wash me, and I will be whiter than snow.
Let me hear joy and gladness;
let the bones you have crushed rejoice.
Hide your face from my sins
and blot out all my iniquity.
Create in me a pure heart, O God,
and renew a steadfast spirit within me.
Do not cast me from your presence
or take your Holy Spirit from me.
Restore to me the joy of your salvation
and grant me a willing spirit, to sustain me. (Ps 51:1-12)
If we do this we cannot fail to be overwhelmed by the cost of forgiveness. Those who will see God are the pure in heart who

mourn over their sin.[8] A prayer-enabled vision of God is never attained by eyes which have not known such tears. *Effective prayer begins with confession* offered by one who knows genuine contrition. There is no other way.[9] "This is what the LORD, the God of your father David, says: 'I have heard your prayer and seen your tears; I will heal you' " (2 Kings 20:5).

Can't You Say Something More Positive?

Holiness is positive. And positive holiness is directly related to prayer: it is the righteous person whom James 5:16 says is powerful and effective in prayer. Christians have been commanded to *be* holy, and this is not accomplished merely by not being unholy. Our salvation even reflects this: having our sins expiated and God's wrath propitiated by Christ's blood does not qualify us for heaven. God has also counted or "imputed" to believers the positive righteousness and holiness of Christ. Thus Christians are called saints (positive holy ones), not merely forgiven "moral neutrals."

For this reason Paul explained the Christian's purpose for existence in positive terms: "We are God's workmanship, created in Christ Jesus to do good works, which God prepared in advance for us to do" (Eph 2:10). And Jesus summarizes the distinctive mark of a Christian as the positive command to love one another as he has loved us (Jn 13:34-35).

I've always felt certain that Jesus was an attractive, capable and strong person who knew where he was going and what he was here for. In short, he had all the marks of that kind of greatness we associate with being a "winner." He probably would *not* have been asked to be in an ad for Breck shampoo, but his strong personal power did allow him to hold together the likes of such violently opposed men as Matthew the tax collector and Simon the zealot.

Nevertheless, Christians often seem to twist our Lord into a wonderful wimp—a ridiculous distortion no one would make had Jesus been an all-pro linebacker, prizefighter or Medal of Honor winner. The resulting view of holiness insults everything Christ lived and died for. Holiness incarnate—the Lord Jesus himself—is positive and attractive, and following him always takes the best and strongest efforts any man or woman is capable of.

We've forgotten that his final word (Jn 16:33) before he did the toughest thing *any* man ever did was "Take heart! I have overcome the world." And we pale before opportunities to take a positive stand for right in the face of evil as if it were a lie that "the one who is in you is greater than the one who is in the world" (1 Jn 4:4).

Ask God to give you this positive image of holiness and its absolutely *certain* conquest over evil. Part of the reason the devil finds us such easy pickings is that the state of the world and our own spiritual reverses can convince us that effort invested in holiness just gets swallowed by a black hole. People demoralized spiritually are easy to demoralize in other ways. Adopt Paul's realistic, biblical approach to holiness:

> Not that I have . . . already been made perfect, but I press on to take hold of that for which Christ Jesus took hold of me. Brothers, I do not consider myself yet to have taken hold of it. But one thing I do: Forgetting what is behind and straining toward what is ahead, I press on toward the goal to win the prize for which God has called me heavenward in Christ Jesus. (Phil 3:12-14)

Zest for life and zeal for holiness go together. It is a *lie*—right out of the pit of hell itself—that holiness and drabness or mediocrity have anything to do with each other. Jesus said, "I have come that they may have life, and have it to the full" (Jn 10:10). Act like the holy one (saint) God has made you in Christ. You'll *never* experience holiness or effective prayer just standing there. Get going! "Pursue righteousness, faith, love and peace, along with those who call on the Lord out of a pure heart" (2 Tim 2:22).

To Sum Up

I have no doubt that most Christians who read this book long for more zest in their prayer time. However, I know of no significant spiritual revival which was not preceded by: (1) an increased awareness of the blinding whiteness of God's holiness; (2) a consequent desire by God's children to repent of and confess their sin; and (3) a firm resolution, with God's help and the encouragement of others, to pursue righteousness, faith, love and peace. These characteristics are what it means to "call on the Lord out of a pure heart."

Why so much on holiness in a book on prayer? Because God *is* holy. Persons not praying on his wavelength—or talking with static on the line—have trouble communicating: they cannot understand what he is saying.[10]

Questions for Thought and Discussion

1. Can you think of illustrations which would either establish or disprove the author's idea that Christians tend to think holiness is primarily a (negative) matter of not being bad, rather than (positively) being good?

2. Why do goody-goody Christians turn people off?

3. How do you explain the fact that Jesus was holy, yet had friendships with drunks, gluttons and prostitutes?

4. The author claims that black clothes and long faces are not the best way to express holiness. What do you think? Does clothing or facial expression have *anything* to do with holiness? Why or why not?

5. Have you ever known any persons who seemed truly holy? What were they like? Had they suffered significantly? Would you say their lives were attractive?

6. What pressures toward unholiness do you face on a typical workday? How about on weekends? How can Christians help one another to be holy?

7. What do you think about the quotation from John Owen on p. 26?

8. Why is it hard to repent of a sin?

9. Why does God want you to be holy?

3
All-Knowing: What Is There to Tell Him?

We received the sample packet of shampoo not too long after I passed my fortieth birthday. The makers claimed it was "specifically formulated" to combat "tired hair"—a condition common on heads which were forty years and older. I was astounded. How did they know I would never see thirty-nine again? Maybe they were told about that party when I was taken under false pretenses to a room decorated with black balloons where my "friends," wearing black arm bands, had gathered to celebrate my passing—into middle age. Did they know about the creaky rocker, the woolen shawl, the tepid foot bath I endured that night? Had they heard the laughter as I opened box after box filled with denture cleansers, liniments, magnifying glasses, or the application to reserve a bed in a nursing home, the booklet about plots with a beautiful view and perpetual care at Forest Lawn? *How did they know?*

The same question, How does he know? arises whenever theologians start talking about God's omniscience. But despite our questions, the statements of Scripture are crystal clear: God knows absolutely everything. The concept is staggering, beyond parallel in human experience.

Some people think a computer provides an apt analogy for God's knowledge because computer "brains" are so big and quick—and no computer ever forgot to pick up a loaf of bread on the way home. But computers are dependent on operator commands and have to be manufactured, programmed and given data. God has always existed, can never be programmed, and knows all the data innately and intrinsically. Nothing is in memory or storage either: he is simultaneously conscious of everything at the same time. And God does not have to be plugged in. But most importantly, God is not an electromechanical machine. His knowledge is not a mass of binary numbers, electromagnetic pulses or synthesized chirps and bleeps. He knows us not as ciphers which originate and terminate, but as children whom he loves. The point is not just that God knows everything, or even that he knows everything *about* us. Rather, it is that he knows *us*—individually and personally—and far better than we know ourselves. You cannot pray to a personal computer no matter how "user friendly" it is.

Nor is God the *Mind*—a disembodied metaphysical deity whose only claim to fame is naked intellect, an infinitely fat head. Yet such a god has haunted the neurons of both Christian heresy and non-Christian error for centuries. Every age has had its gnostics (from the Greek word *gnosis,* meaning "knowledge") who worship not God, but what they wish they knew. Divinity for them is an abstract and impersonal wisdom.

With such a Mind, one may contemplate, seek to merge one's thoughts, or seek fuller and higher levels of esoteric comprehension of the truth. But one cannot communicate with it. You may say things such as, "O holy Knowledge, by thee I am illumined and through thee do I sing praise to the incorporeal Light."[1] But you cannot ask for help in coping with your mother-in-law or give thanks for a piece of chocolate cake to an Idea. The divine Mind is nonpersonal and nameless. It may be spoken at—but not spoken to. The text just quoted is ancient, but such notions live on.[2] And as we now live in a world which increasingly worships—not just manages—information, the cult of the divine Mind will prosper. The personal God Christians call Father transcends characterization as an abstract absolute intelligence. Fortunately, God is not just the heavenly Head either.

When a Christian says, "Lord, you know all things," the one spoken to *is* infinite Wisdom, Understanding, Intellect, Knowledge, Rationality and the Source of all Truth. But at the same time he is also the "Wonderful Counselor, Mighty God, Everlasting Father, Prince of Peace" (Is 9:6). And that makes all the difference.

The God Who Knows Me
Scripture contains many statements which assert God's knowledge about us. Some are general: "The eyes of the LORD are in every place, keeping watch on the evil and the good" (Prov 15:3 RSV); others are more specific: "The ways of a man are before the eyes of the LORD, and He watches all his paths" (Prov 5:21 NASB). A few make God's knowledge seem remote. But the most famous is intensely personal:

O LORD, you have searched me
    and you know me.
You know when I sit and when I rise;
    you perceive my thoughts from afar.
You discern my going out and my lying down;
    you are familiar with all my ways.
Before a word is on my tongue
    you know it completely, O LORD.
You hem me in—behind and before;
    you have laid your hand upon me.
Such knowledge is too wonderful for me,

too lofty for me to attain.
Where can I go from your Spirit?
    Where can I flee from your presence?
If I go up to the heavens, you are there;
    if I make my bed in the depths, you are there.
If I rise on the wings of the dawn,
    if I settle on the far side of the sea,
even there your hand will guide me,
    your right hand will hold me fast.
If I say, "Surely the darkness will hide me
    and the light become night around me,"
even the darkness will not be dark to you;
    the night will shine like the day,
    for darkness is as light to you. (Ps 139:1-12)

The last half of this passage adds to the idea of God's omniscience
(knowledge of all) the thought of his omnipresence (presence everywhere). God's omnipresence is an important concept because Scripture says the Creator is in some sense present throughout the
whole of his creation. This does not mean that God is *contained* in
or by the creation. (The latter idea is found in many Eastern relig-
ions.)

According to Scripture, the Maker of heaven and earth is present
throughout his creation, but he is distinct from it. The Father fills
heaven and earth (Jer 23:24); the Son, the Lord Jesus, is with us
always (Mt 28:20) and upholds all things (Heb 1:3; Col 1:17); and
there is, as David said, nowhere you can flee from the Holy Spirit
(Ps 139:7). The God Christians pray to is always there—everywhere. And because we are creatures locked in both time and space,
God's omnipresence is also incomprehensible.

Where Can I Flee . . . ?

Many of us don't think too often about God's omniscience or omnipresence. The words are a mouthful and part of a scholarly discipline that is not part of our daily lives. We don't think much about
photosensitivity, thermodynamic heat transfer or hydraulic pres-

sure most days either. But if I say, "It was dark, her hand felt warm and his pulse rate was rising," all three ideas become a little more personal. The Bible does this sort of illustrating—the authors explaining abstract concepts like omniscience and omnipresence with the sort of living language David uses in Psalm 139. Jeremiah is understandable to any child who has played hide-and-seek:

"Am I only a God nearby,"
   declares the LORD,
   "and not a God far away?
Can anyone hide in secret places
   so that I cannot see him?" (Jer 23:23-24)

But despite such clarity and vividness, we still try to forget that God is everywhere and knows everything. One reason is that if God is really like this, then there is no place to hide. You can *never* get away from him. And this idea is a threat. Imagine: you can't "sneak" anything past him; *he knows all.* And he is always there, even when you're alone in the dark with the doors locked. Yes, David's thought, "you hem me in," can be comforting. Most of us feel the need for outside help occasionally. But we also know we have secret sins and moral irregularities; we turn our back on numberless opportunities to do good. So feeling there is nowhere to hide from God's searching eye can be oppressive. "Nothing in all creation is hidden from God's sight. Everything is uncovered and laid bare before the eyes of him to whom we must give account" (Heb 4:13).

We find it easy to keep ideas like God's omniscience and omnipresence stashed safely away with other curious and dusty oddities on that mental shelf called Interesting Theological Truth. It's a simple matter of self-defense. You just sort of, well . . . forget it. And then there are, of course, parts of the Bible which will actually help us do it. And we hear those (comforting) words nearly every week—when we worship.

Let Us Come Before His Presence
I do not know the number of times I have sung the words of Habakkuk 2:20, "The Lord is in His holy temple. Let all the earth be

silent before Him" (NASB). Images of God on his throne, such as those in Isaiah 6 and Revelation 4, are an important part of the Christian worship tradition. But the image left by such texts is that God is localized in the place where his people gather to worship and pray. And this picture of God sticks in our minds. Our own experience reinforces this image. Day in, day out we operate on the supposition that it is good that God is sitting on his throne in his holy temple: it keeps him out of the way and lets us get on with our lives.

It seems obvious: if we come *into* God's presence in worship and prayer, we must walk *out of* God's presence when the service or prayer meeting is over. Are we conscious of God's presence on the beach, at the factory, in a store, in our office or fighting the traffic on the freeway? Where is God when we wax the bathroom floor, have an argument with our kids, or change the plugs in the car? Where is he when we kiss our spouse, check out groceries or take out the garbage? He is in his holy temple, isn't he? Sure, God is in a box: a *very* beautiful and dignified—don't run in the sanctuary—*box*. But it is an isolation compartment just the same. There is the "sacred" and the "secular." There is theology, and there is reality. There is the holy temple, and there is the real world—the joys and traumas of life.

While this kind of unconscious deception is wrong, it is also very old among the people of God. Solomon, who dedicated God's first holy Temple in Jerusalem, worried about it, asking: "But will God really dwell on earth? The heavens, even the highest heaven, cannot contain you. How much less this temple I have built!" (1 Kings 8:27). And God asked through Isaiah, "Where is the house you will build for me?" (66:1).

The problem is universal; Paul found the same thinking in Athens among the sophisticated and civic leaders near the apex of paganism. He said pointedly, "The God who made the world and everything in it is the Lord of heaven and earth and *does not live in temples built by hands*" (Acts 17:24). Irrespective of whether we continue in the superstition that God is more interested in the spiritual exercises we think of as "sacred" than he is in the vast bulk of our "secular" life experiences—the working, frustrating, exhilarating, frightening, loving, boring stuff of which most days consist—he is *still* there, aware and caring about everything and anything we do, say or think.

Practicing the presence of God, thinking and living as if he *is* always really there, takes significant conscious effort. Not only do your presuppositions work against you, but nearly every inch of the way you also have to swim upstream against the current of modern life.

Living in Compartments
The phenomenon I have in mind sociologists call the fragmentation of life. For very few is life still organized around the farm, fishing boat or flock. Now we jump from box to box driven by the clock. Join me as we follow Pilgrim's progress.

Christian begins the day with a "quiet time" followed immediately by a shower, the working clothes, a rushed breakfast and a kiss on the cheek. If the children are up, add optional bathroom jam.

Next comes the commute: ten to a hundred minutes by bike, car, bus or train. Off to work, but not so fast: jam not optional.

Most of Christian's energy is expended here on the job, away from home with different people, goals and experiences. Even the language, the jargon of the job, is different.

Next comes the return trip. Miles of asphalt, concrete and steel.

Back home Christian enters the world of household joys and problems. (On the way out in the morning he just passes through.) The atmosphere is again different. There are lawns to mow, children to bathe and talk about school, who gets the car tonight and utility bills.

But tonight is Wednesday. So it's back in the car for more asphalt and concrete. It takes 20 minutes to get to the prayer meeting at church.

Christian now enters a third world. The people are mostly different, conversation takes a particular bent and there is another distinct jargon to keep track of. It's time to pray. God, it seems, lives in another world—sixteenth-century Britain. He is addressed as an Elizabethan Englishman, and when around him it's apparently wise to keep a stiff upper lip.

The meeting is over and it's back in the car again. The older kids went to an amusement park and it's Christian's turn to pick them up on the way home. More miles of steel guard rails and flashing lights.

At the park now, Christian enters the thrill-a-minute unreality of modern fantasy and hype. The place is crawling with yet another clan of people and filled with unique sights, sounds and smells. All are cheerfully catered to by the clean scrubbed faces of a staff having perpetual youth.

Back to the car. What a faithful steed! Only twelve and three-fourths miles to drop them all off. Then Christian tonight no more you will need.

Home at last, Christian is near collapse. Sleep finally overtakes our saint while watching the TV late news. The day ends in a world all its own: Disaster and détente discussed by a man trying hard to look concerned, the latest in mushroom brushes—absolutely fascinating to the girl with those long lashes—and the fellow with the orange bow tie smiling in front of photos of a typhoon near Hawaii.

Not you? O.K., and I'm glad. But life is like this for millions. You can change the events and destinations, substitute bass fishing, quilt making, racquetball or putting up the storm windows. But life consists of a sequence of quite different places, roles and language requirements through which Christians are forced by family goals, peer pressure, insecurity and their digital watches.

And we are told that these worlds, these boxes, must be kept separate: "Leave your job problems at work," or, "Don't let domestic strife affect the quality of your work." And every Christian knows you can never tell anyone at church what is *really* going on at home or the office. Life is almost forced into a series of sealed compartments.

Look, the drapes are parting! The man says, "This is *your* life."

"Looks like a TV dinner," you say.

"Right!" the man says. "This *is* your life."

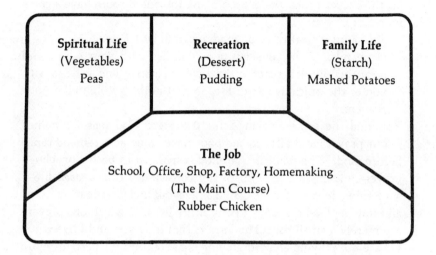

Getting It All Together

So what has this got to do with prayer and God's omniscience and omnipresence? Quite a bit. Though we go from compartment to compartment in a kind of tour through the TV dinner of our lives, for God things aren't separated by aluminum foil or miles of free-way or by time or distance or anything else. For God your life is a kind of chicken pot pie. *Everything* in it relates to all the other parts; the flavors interact. Too much or not enough of any ingredient can affect the whole lot. There are no sacred and secular compartments. It is all part of what he sees . . . and what he reacts to when you pray.

God does not just hear your prayers. He "hears" your whole life. He doesn't respond to what you *say*. He responds to what you *are*. He responds to you. You are the factor that ties all the boxes, the compartments together. It may be difficult to see how what happened in your quiet time this morning can be related to your prayer two days ago about a problem you expect with the boss after lunch tomorrow. But to an omniscient, omnipresent God it all fits together: the prayer room, the bedroom and the board room have a common factor, you.

This point is confirmed beyond question by 1 Peter 3:7.

> Husbands, . . . be considerate as you live with your wives, and treat them with respect as the weaker partner, and as heirs with you of the gracious gift of life, so that nothing will hinder your prayers.

You find the same idea in Acts 10:4. Here God tells Cornelius, "Your prayers and gifts to the poor have come as a remembrance before God." The point is that God responded to both Cornelius's prayers and his almsgiving, to the consistency of his *whole* life—something described in Acts 10:2 as "devout and God-fearing." Our all-knowing God responds to our entire lives, of which our prayers are merely a small part. This means that how you and I live when we are not praying and worshiping is as significant—perhaps more so—than when we do.

The Old Testament patriarch Jacob once said, "Surely the LORD is in this place, and I did not know it" (Gen 28:16 NASB). And every Christian must recognize that the structure of existence in the modern world almost contrives to suppress this essential truth about our all-present God. One of the major reasons why we must see our whole lives as an act of prayer is because it seems certain that God can look at us no other way. Because he is there, *all* of life is sacred.

So What Do You Want Me to Do?

Holiness, wholeness, honesty and hope: these words summarize the practical implications of my point. *Holiness* has already been given a chapter of its own. Yet comprehending God's omniscience must underscore the necessity of the prayer of confession. David, who wrote Psalm 139, said, "Search me, O God, and know my heart; test me and know my anxious thoughts. See if there is any offensive way in me, and lead me in the way everlasting" (vv. 23-24).

Wholeness lies in the fact that an all-knowing Lord cares about everything you say, do and think. Consequently, you can pray anytime, anywhere and any way. Prayer in the coffee shop is as effective as prayer in any cathedral. Despite the behavior and intonation of religious professionals like me, there is *no* sacred language or ritual which gets God's attention. He hears you no matter how you pray. You already had his attention before you were even born (Ps 139:16).

With this kind of advanced booking, you are obviously not going to pray anything without finding God in the audience. Pray what is on your heart, the best way you can. He asks nothing else from any woman or man.

Honesty is plainly related to God's omniscience in many ways. You cannot lie to Someone who already knows the whole truth. You can lie to yourself, or the others you may pray with, but not to the Lord.

But *what can you tell God, if he already knows everything?* This is a common thought among Christians, especially in the West, because our pragmatism and logic force us to the certain answer: *nothing.* And a formidable array of biblical texts can be advanced in support (for example, Mt 6:8; Eph 1:11; 3:20). You can easily envision God being interrupted by you as he manages the universe and saying into the phone: "It's been good to hear from you, kid. But listen. Next time, don't call Me, I'll call you."

But the Bible is fundamentally an Eastern, specifically, a Semitic book written largely by men who were neither pragmatists nor slaves of Western logic.[3] When Jesus the Semite spoke of God's omniscience he clearly thought it would encourage, *not* discourage, his Semitic disciples to pray. In Matthew 6 he says that our Father already knows what we need before we ask him, and he concludes: this is how we should pray. Westerners scratch their cerebral lobes at this sort of conclusion. But Jesus' logic is flawless and extremely practical. It is as silly as asking for bananas in a hardware store to ask God for something he doesn't have. Because your heavenly Father knows before you ask, he never gets surprised by your re-

quest and finds it necessary to send you a form letter saying your
answer is back-ordered. He already has everything you will ever
need. If God does not answer your petition, it is not because what
you asked for is out of stock.

In Matthew 6 Christ points out that God's children do not have
to get his attention through ostentation (vv. 5-6) or senseless repe-
tition (v. 7). God's children are already objects of his concern before
they pray, and so they can freely ask him for what they need.

In Luke 12:6 Jesus tells us, "Are not five sparrows sold for two
cents? And yet not one of them is forgotten before God" (NASB).
The thought is completed in Matthew 10:30-31: "But the very hairs
of your head are all numbered. Therefore do not fear; you are of
more value than many sparrows" (NASB).[4] Why on earth does God
keep track of his children's hair? For the same reason we do. Jo-Ann
and I have two small, clear plastic vials in the hall closet. One contains a clipping from my son's first haircut, the other several curls
of the blond fluff his sister was born with. Their hair is part of the
children we cherish. And we "keep track of it" because we love
them. Likewise, God knows and cares even about the smallest
things; since you are so greatly valued and loved, you don't have to
be afraid. Jesus sees God's omniscience as logically leading to *freedom*
from fear.

Consider again our question: What can you tell God if he knows
everything? And notice the opposite conclusions:

Western logic: Nothing.

Jesus: Anything.

The point is that since God already knows *everything* about you and
still loves you, then there is *nothing* you can tell him that will change
his feelings for you. He is obviously not a Self-righteous Celestial
Prude, but a loving Father who hugs his children—even when they
have jam on their faces. The upshot of this is absolute *certainty* that
nothing you ever tell God will cause him to turn his back on you.
Seen this way, God's omniscience is not a liability, it is the source
of interpersonal liberation.

Told some secret sin, the Father does not recoil (hand to mouth) in shock. Nor does he wonder, "How are we ever going to pull this one out of the fire?" There is no eyebrow-raising condescension when you express your inadequacies, and he doesn't sigh and say, "Well, you'll *just* have to be more patient," when you seethe with frustration. His reply is the calm reassurance we all ache for but so rarely find: "I know, I know, I understand."

Is there really anyone you feel you can approach with absolute transparency—with complete honesty? Some couples find it with each other and a few have such a friend. But I am certain that thousands upon thousands feel there is no one whom they can trust enough simply to be themselves. God *is* such a person—because he knows and loves and because Jesus died for you. You may feel you must pretend with your priest, your minister, your elder, maybe even your mother. But not so with your heavenly Father.

In our Lord we have someone with whom we can share our anger, joy, *fear*, frustration, delight, endless struggles with sin, hurt, loneliness—our real selves. This is the powerful liberating honesty which should result from understanding God's omniscience. With God, we can be somebody: ourself; we don't have to be somebody else. And God also cares about our aspirations—something the twisted self-deprecation which passes among Christians as humility has wrongly convinced us we are not supposed to have. Tell God your dreams, goals, hopes, the desires you have to make something out of yourself. There is no worm so wretched, but what God cannot glorify himself by making it into a butterfly.

We have learned, I am afraid, to lie to one another as Christians so easily that the concept of being honest with God may seem funny. I admit to being able to respond to the question, "How are you?" with the lie, "Just fine, thanks. How are you?" even on days when I feel terrible and wish the cheery inquirer would go away. As a "professional Christian" I'm expected to always be fine . . . thanks. So I often say I am . . . even when I'm not. But I realize increasingly that keeping spiritual reality and what we have convinced ourselves should be spiritual reality—myself and my image, if you like—separate has a tremendous personal cost. If we do this long enough we become a split personality—a kind of spiritual schizophrenic. Our relationship with others becomes increasingly unsatisfying, and we often end up trying to tell God, "Just fine, thanks," too. Being honest with God is the first step toward being honest with ourselves. And if we are not transparent in these two areas it is hard to be anything but opaque when talking with others. Honesty with God in prayer is essential to personal and spiritual wholeness. What God doesn't know can't hurt him? You're right. There isn't anything he doesn't know. It's you who gets hurt. There is no joy in any relationship which must maintain deception—even if it is self-deception. Eventually we start avoiding the tension by avoiding God.

God loves *you* more than you will ever know. Not your image, not your happy face, not your spirituality—but you. The real you. The one you think nobody knows about. No, real love is *not* blind. Because his eyes are open, he can see what you cannot. And he felt what he saw in you was worth dying for. So when you pray be honest. Tell him everything.

The final word I linked with God's omniscience and omnipresence was *hope*. Because God is omniscient he knows enough to do what is both right and best. Because we are so limited much of what happens will, until it happens, be unknown. But because God is omnipresent, as children of God we never face the unknown alone. These two facts are essential to Christian hope, trust and faith. They are essential to prayer when we cannot understand what our Father is doing. When we don't get what we ask for, when the future holds things we don't understand, when there seems to be no future, God is always there. If we cannot comprehend the mind of the Lord, we *have* known the love of the Lord. And where there is love, there is hope. "No mind has conceived what God has prepared for those who love him" (1 Cor 2:9).

Questions for Thought and Discussion

1. If you can, describe your personal feelings in response to the statement from Hebrews 4:13 that "nothing in all creation is hidden from God's sight."

2. What aspects of your life, if any, do you wish could be hidden from God's sight? Why do you feel this way?

3. Is the author right in contending that special places of prayer and worship make us prone to "keep God in a box"? Do you think it is significant that God commanded Israel only to build a portable tabernacle or mobile tent? How would you feel if God were "camping out" next to your house?

4. The author contends that the modern Christian life often is a series of compartments. Is life really as fragmented as he suggests? In what way is your life fragmented?

5. Do you think it is right to say that all of life is sacred? Why or why not?

6. Why does a cathedral often seem a better place for prayer than a coffee shop?

7. Do you ever feel you have to pretend with other believers? Do you think they would accept you just as you are?

8. Do you feel free to tell God everything? What seems "off limits"?

4
Sovereign: Can Prayer Change God's Mind?

At its root, prayer grows from the certainty of God's omnipotence and sovereignty. Job says, "I know that you can do all things; no plan of yours can be thwarted" (42:2). Obviously it would be a waste of time to pray to a wimp.

Take the simple petition, "Please don't let it rain on my birthday." If your birthday is the 17th, and God desires it not to rain on your party in the park, it may be necessary to change a high-pressure system 246 miles wide, 28,546 feet above the middle of the Pacific Ocean, and that must be done eleven days *before* you prayed about it on the 15th.[1] The effect this may have afterward on weather elsewhere in the world has also got to be taken into consideration. We tend to forget things like these because thermodynamics, not theology, is the basis of modern meteorology. And, as has often been said, it is very easy to think God does nothing because he does certain things often. But natural processes that we have come to think of as routine or simple are the result of, and are sustained (or changed) by, God's power.

To be worth praying to, God has first of all got to have the power to do what we ask. Second, he must have sovereignty over creation to do what he wants to do. Imagine a being who responded to your birthday prayer with, "Well, you see, I'd really like to make it sunny for you; it's no problem at all to do it, but I just can't. It's like this sometimes, and I can't do anything about it. I'm really frustrated as much as you are. I'm so sorry. Maybe tomorrow? Well, I just don't know."

I am glad the God Christians pray to is both omnipotent and sovereign. The psalmist says, "He does whatever pleases him" (115:3). The theme is amplified in Daniel 4:35:

He does as he pleases
 with the powers of heaven
 and the peoples of the earth.
No one can hold back his hand
 or say to him: "What have you done?"

And God's power and authority are eternal: "Your kingdom is an everlasting kingdom, and your dominion endures through all generations" (Ps 145:13).

But is someone with absolute, eternal sovereignty and power necessarily *friendly?* The answer is no. Imagine your birthday supplication being bashed back: "Look, whatever I choose to do is O.K., see? I'm the Boss . . . and don't you ever forget it . . . (I can't). I make the rules around here . . . (and everywhere else). You've got no choice but to see it my way and accept whatever I do. That's the way things are . . . (and ever shall be . . . it'll never end). Stop asking questions. You want to get zapped or something? Get out of here and stop bothering me. You can't even imagine what I've got up my sleeve. It's my universe, and I'll do what I want with it."

This is "god-father" all right, but hardly the good Father who sent his Son to die for us. For prayer to make sense, God's omnipotence and sovereignty must be coupled with his goodness and moral perfection. Christians pray to a God whose every act is always kind and who does nothing from mere whim or arbitrary caprice. Thus Jesus says,

> Which of you, if his son asks for bread, will give him a stone? Or if he asks for a fish, will give him a snake? If you, then, though you are evil, know how to give good gifts to your children, how much more will your Father in heaven give good gifts to those who ask him! (Mt 7:9-11)

Taken together, the ideas of God's omnipotence, sovereignty and goodness are the primary basis for what Christian scholars call providence. The term is defined by J. I Packer as "the unceasing activity of the Creator whereby, in overflowing bounty and goodwill . . . He upholds His creatures in ordered existence, . . . guides and governs all events, circumstances, and free acts of angels and men, . . . and directs everything to its appointed goal, for His own glory."[2]

Packer has merely summarized what Scripture says about God and his relationship to his creation.[3] In fact, in theological literature it is common to find *providence* used as a synonym for God. Because of God's providential care for his creation, ultimately, there is no such thing as luck. What is more, from God's perspective, there are not really any accidents, surprises or "curious turns of history." What we call chance doesn't exist. Sound extreme? Yes it does. But these ideas are straightforward consequences of verses like Proverbs 16:33: "The lot is cast into the lap, but its every decision is from the LORD" (NASB). From a biblical perspective, your world-history book should be prefaced with 2 Kings 19:25, "Have you not heard? Long ago I ordained it. In the days of old I planned it; now I have brought it to pass."

But Surely Everything Changes in Time

This last quoted text will trouble some and raise questions for nearly everybody. It suggests: (1) God has always known what he wished to have happened ("I planned it"); (2) God does not change his mind about what he planned; and hence (3) God causes or permits things to happen ("I have brought it to pass"). Other texts seem to say the same thing:

> Known unto God from eternity are all his works. (Acts 15:18 KJV)

> Remember the former things of old;
> for I am God, and there is no other;
>   I am God, and there is none like me,
> declaring the end from the beginning
>   and from ancient times things not yet done,
> saying, "My counsel shall stand,
>   and I will accomplish all my purpose," . . .
> I have spoken, and I will bring it to pass;
>   I have purposed, and I will do it. (Is 46:9-11 RSV)

These kinds of words about God's eternal, immutable will raise a lot of questions, especially about prayer. Why pray at all? Asking God for things seems silly. My prayers tell him nothing he doesn't already know; I can't change his mind; and since he knows what is best, he will do what he wants anyway. Yet the authors of Scripture were intelligent men to whom such problems can hardly have been unknown. And they were men who prayed. Isaiah and Paul are good examples. It was Isaiah who said to Hezekiah: "This is what the Lord says, 'Put your house in order, because you are going to die: you will not recover' " (Is 38:1). And after the king had wept bitterly and prayed about his impending doom, it was Isaiah—who had not even gotten out of the king's house after delivering the Lord's sentence of death—whom God told: "Go back and tell Hezekiah . . . 'This is what the LORD, the God of your father David says, "I have heard your prayer and seen your tears; I will heal you. . . . I will add fifteen years to your life" ' " (2 Kings 20:5-6). The prophet's own account makes it plain that had the king not prayed, he would have died (Is 38:1-22).

Paul, for his part, says more about God's eternal election and predestination unto salvation than any other biblical writer. In Romans 9—11 he applies this doctrine to Israel, his own race. In 9:16 he says that salvation does not depend on man's desire or effort, a statement which seems to preclude prayer. And the chapter as a whole makes it certain that "God has mercy on whom he wants to have mercy" (v. 18). Paul even rebukes the person who might wish to tell God this seems unfair (see esp. vv. 14-21). These themes are repeated again in chapter 11 which concludes with a doxology containing the line: "Who has known the mind of the Lord? Or who has been his counselor?" (v. 34). Man's complete nonparticipation in human salvation seems obvious: God saves only whom he wants, and what is more, he decided to do it *before* people were "born or had done anything good or bad" (9:11).

Right in the middle of this, Paul says in 10:1, "My heart's desire and *prayer to God* for the Israelites is that they may be saved." It seems certain he would not have spent his time praying about a cause already lost to a God who would not respond to his prayers. Paul vigorously taught God's sovereignty in salvation *and* prayed vigorously for God to save people. He prayed for what he was confident God had already decided to do. For Paul, the priority of God's omnipotence, wisdom, goodness and omniscience—the immutability of his will—seems to encourage prayer rather than make it unnecessary.

Finally, consider Jesus. He knew that by God's set purpose and foreknowledge he would be put to death by being nailed to the cross (Acts 2:23). He told the incredulous disciples this at least three times. (Mark 10:33-34 is an example.) Yet in Gethsemane, as Mark tells it, he "fell to the ground and prayed that if possible the hour might pass from him." (14:35).

The only conclusion to draw from these three people is that they felt that the eternal, immutable, sovereign God responds to prayer. Persons so central in the communication of God's Word to humanity could not be mistaken about this.

We are left with the apparently contradictory assertions that God makes up his own mind and does what he wants, and yet he responds to human prayer. I have no rabbits to pull out of this paradoxical hat. We must face this question squarely.

Does Prayer Change God's Mind?

Exodus 32:9-14 says that in response to prayer God repented, or changed his mind. Moses' famous intercession for Israel after their sin with the golden calf is often cited in books on prayer as an example of the results of fervent prayer on the lips of a righteous and faithful man. So powerful, it is said, are such prayers that they are able to wrest blessing or divert catastrophe from a God reluctant to change his mind once his plan is fixed. But *does* Scripture teach that prayer changes God's mind?

Important orthodox theologians have suggested that "God is the sovereign lord of history to whom at every juncture alternatives remain open."[4] This implies that Exodus 32:14 and similar texts are evidence of "God's freedom to change his mind or the ways in which he deals with his people."[5] But I see it differently.

My conviction is that references to God's "repenting," "relenting" or "changing his mind" in Scripture are figures of speech; technically speaking, they are anthropopathisms—expressions which explain God in terms usually used to describe human emotions.[6] The Bible frequently speaks about God by analogy. But such language cannot be interpreted literally. For example, if God is spirit, as Jesus says in John 4:24, then his is not a physical existence: God the Father does not have a body. Yet biblical authors repeatedly describe his activity using figures of speech (anthropomorphisms) which are analogies to the human body. In Isaiah 40, for example, God is said to have a "hand" (vv. 2, 12); "mouth" (v. 5); "breath" (v. 7); "arm" (vv. 10-11) and "heart" (v. 11).

Similarly, I believe God's "repentance" is an anthropopathism because the Bible explicitly says God does *not* change his mind: "God is not a man . . . that He should repent" (Num 23:19 NASB); "The Glory of Israel will not . . . change his mind; for He is not a man that He should change His mind" (1 Sam 15:29 NASB). What then does Exodus 32:14 mean?

Alan Cole comments on God's response to Moses' prayer:

The meaning is not that God changed His mind; still less that He regretted something that He had intended to do. It means, in biblical language, that He now embarked on a different course of action from that already suggested as a possibility, owing to some new factor which is usually mentioned in the context. In the Bible, it is clear that God's promises and warnings are always conditional on man's response: this is most clearly set out in Ezekiel 33:13-16. We are not to think of Moses as altering God's purpose towards Israel by this prayer, but as carrying it out: Moses was never more like God than in such moments, for he shared God's mind and loving purpose.[7]

Consider Jacob's statement in Genesis 49:10: "The scepter will not depart from Judah, nor the ruler's staff from between his feet, until he comes to whom it belongs." This has often been taken as a prophetic promise by God concerning the kingly line in Israel and the Messiah's descent from the tribe of Judah. (Matthew 1:3 confirms that the latter took place.) Moses was of the tribe of Levi, not Judah (Ex 2:1-9). God suggests to Moses in Exodus 32:10, after the people's sin, that he will destroy the nation and make from Moses a great nation. The kings and Messiah would thus have to come through Moses' line, not Judah's. Since God's promises are certain, I take it that if Genesis 49:10 is prophetic, then God did *not* plan to destroy Israel—at least not *all* of the tribe of Judah— though his statement in Exodus 32:10 suggests the possibility to Moses. I conclude that Moses did not change God's mind when he prayed. He pleaded for what God had always intended to do. If the man who talked to God "face to face" (Ex 33:11) did not change God's mind, I think it unlikely we will.

Gotcha!

Some readers, having read the previous section, are now probably thinking: "You're a slippery one. But I've gotcha now! My prayers don't really matter one bit as far as what God does.[8] And you've just proved it by saying Moses didn't change God's mind in Exodus 32:14." My response: Don't bail out yet. Stay with me a minute longer before you chuck the book and turn on the TV.

In both testaments God *commands* his people to pray. Does he do this only because it is psychologically healthy to ventilate our feelings? Does the One who commands us to redeem the time want us to waste it in an activity which is ultimately pointless? Why does Scripture repeatedly assert that God hears petition and responds to supplication if he doesn't? Is it possible human prayer is somehow essential to the accomplishment of God's sovereign will . . . even if we cannot hold that it changes God's will?

Your prayers *do* matter. If you take the Bible seriously, there is no other conclusion which can be drawn. The question is, *How* do our prayers matter? How do they relate to God's sovereign, eternal purposes?

We will never fully understand God's ways (see, for example, Job 11:7-8; Is 55:8-9). Comprehending the relationship between our prayers and God's purposes will probably strain your thinking as much as it does mine. A certain incomprehensibility results whenever one sets out to explain the places in history and theology where humanity and divinity come in contact. The ancient debate about the full humanity and complete divinity of the Lord Jesus, and the modern argument about the role of fallible men in writing the infallible Word of God are two obvious examples. And we must be wary of cut-and-dried solutions to any biblical paradox. The "definitive" resolution of the issue is known to God, who has wisely chosen not to blow our brains by telling us what it is. Both faith and experience say prayer matters, and human petition and immutable divine sovereignty must somehow "fit" together.

A popular point of view is that human prayer is needed so that God can accomplish what he has already purposed to do. S. D. Gordon wrote:

Everything that has ever been prayed for, of course I mean every right thing, God has already purposed to do. But He does nothing without consent. He has been hindered in His purpose by our lack of willingness. When we learn His purposes and make them our prayers, we are giving Him an opportunity to act.[9]

Gordon did not shrink, in fact, from saying that people are damned to hell because Christians do not pray for their salvation: "There are people . . . in that lower, lost world . . . who are there . . . because someone failed to put his life in touch with God, and pray."[10]

Gordon's view assumes that God has self-limited his sovereignty so as to make accomplishment of aspects of his will dependent on prayer. God is said to be ready and willing to bless (or save) men and women, but he cannot do so unless through prayer they indicate their willingness for him to do so.[11] This would mean that unless we pray, God cannot accomplish his purposes in the world. Prayer thus becomes necessary in an *absolute* sense: God is powerless to act without our prayers.

Gordon's view has been held by Christians for decades. It has tremendous emotional appeal and motivates one to pray both long and fervently. But I am not convinced by it. This view makes the sovereign, omnipotent Creator dependent on the consent and willingness of his sinful, fallible creatures. Daniel 4:35 says, "No one can hold back his hand." But this conflicts directly with Gordon's assertion that God "has been hindered in his purpose by our lack of willingness." Romans 9:15 ("I will have mercy on whom I will have mercy, and I will have compassion on whom I have compassion") hardly seems to make receiving God's mercy in salvation dependent on whether someone put his life in touch with God through prayer. Scripture forces me to conclude that Gordon's view is inadequate.

Can You Come Up with Anything Better?
It seems better to think that prayer has been ordained by God as a means to accomplish aspects of his will. Given human limitation, God must do many things irrespective of whether or how people pray. Nevertheless, apparently there are some activities which God has chosen to accomplish in a way which allows men and women to cooperate through prayer in bringing his will to fruition. God gives his children the impulse and ability to pray in order that he

may respond to their petitions and carry out aspects of his will.[12]

Prayers are the free acts of men and women, and God is not dependent on or limited by them. But he is pleased to bring his purposes into reality by responding to prayer. This view is supported by texts such as the following: "In his heart a man plans his course, but the LORD determines his steps" (Prov 16:9); "It is God who works in you to will and to act according to his good purpose" (Phil 2:13). The best biblical illustration is probably found in Ezekiel 36. This chapter is saturated with assertions about the sovereignty of God. (The NIV uses "Sovereign LORD" fifteen times in thirty-eight verses!) Two verses here make God's sovereignty especially explicit: "This is what the Sovereign LORD says: It is not for your sake, O house of Israel, that I am going to do these things, but for the sake of my holy name" (v. 22); "I want you to know that I am not doing this for your sake, declares the Sovereign LORD" (v. 32).

God will do what he has sovereignly chosen to do. This thought is the central point of Ezekiel 36. But in the final two verses the sovereign Lord says he will act *in response to the prayers of his people:* "This is what the Sovereign LORD says: Once again I will yield to the plea of the house of Israel and do this for them. . . . Then they will know I am the LORD" (vv. 37-38). So as to act sovereignly, God apparently will move his people to pray so he can respond. The upshot of this process is this:

☐ God is sovereign and unhindered.

☐ We are free; we pray.

☐ His will is done.

☐ His holy name is glorified.

☐ We know that he is the Lord.

I cannot pretend to have proven that this is the only solution to the question posed when we started. But it is a more satisfying and consistently biblical approach than Gordon's alternative. And this approach has appealed to others. C. S. Lewis once said,

Infinite wisdom does not need telling what is best, and infinite goodness needs no urging to do it. But neither does God need any of those things that are done by finite agents, whether living or inanimate. He could, if He chose, repair our bodies miraculously without food; or give us food without the aid of farmers, bakers and butchers; or knowledge without the aid of learned men; or convert the heathen without missionaries. Instead, He allows soils and weather and animals and muscles, minds and wills of men to co-operate in the execution of His Will. "God," said Pascal, "instituted prayer in order to lend to His creatures the dignity of causality."[13]

So Who Wants to Be a Puppet?

A major rub in the "cooperation" approach is the priority of God's will. If God gives us the ability and impulse to pray for what he wants to accomplish, then our prayers are not the free expressions of responsible creatures. They are like the "words" spoken by puppets whose strings are pulled by someone else. This is an old and good objection. But responsible scholars have been convinced for centuries—despite the apparent paradox—that we pray as free agents. J. I. Packer rightly summarizes what Scripture teaches:

> God rules the hearts and actions of all men (cf. Pr. 21:1; Ezr. 6:22), often for purposes of his own which they do not suspect (cf. Gn. 45:5-8; 50:20; Is. 10:5ff; 44:28—45:2; Jn. 11:49ff; Acts 13:27ff). God's control is absolute in the sense that men do only that which he has ordained that they should do; yet they are truly free agents, in the sense that their decisions are their own, and they are morally responsible for them (cf. Dt. 30:15ff).[14]

Nevertheless, it still seems like praying under God's absolute control hardly describes free agents, even if we are morally responsible. It seems as though volitionally we really do nothing.

T. C. Hammond helped me to work through some of the difficulties here. Hammond gives two helpful illustrations concerning God's control and our prayers. It is possible, he says, to think of God as a mother cat who grabs us like a kitten by the back of the neck and carries us willy-nilly wherever she wishes. The kitten is completely passive, its wishes irrelevant to where it is taken. But Hammond finds a more satisfying illustration by looking at a family of monkeys: "The [mother] monkey jumps from branch to branch with its young clinging 'round its neck. The mother monkey does the work, but the young one consciously clings."[15] The little monkey goes where the mother goes because it wants to, and this is what happens when Christians pray according to God's will. What God wants, we want; and we seek to pray according to his will.

Those who deny our active involvement in prayer probably hold a "cat theory" about divine-human relationships. Neither viewpoint puts the little one in control: kittens and little monkeys are both as impotent as men and women are in comparison with God. The difference is the kitten's complete passivity contrasted with the baby monkey's active participation. Similarly, we freely participate in response to the urging of God's Spirit within us when we pray according to the Father's will. Hammond goes on to say:

> God works in us. There is and there must be a human response to the divine overture. That [response] is embodied in Augustine's famous phrase, "Draw us and we will run after Thee." . . .
>
> Prayer . . . is a condition induced of God but indispensable for the performance of His work of grace. Prayer is at once a spiritual condition and evidence of it. The awakened soul cries unto God as naturally as the infant cries for food. Where the cry is lacking, there is danger of death. And the cry brings the answer because the mother-heart is turned to the wail of a babe. Dare we say that God also creates in us this yearning after Him and His will, and is under compulsion of His own nature to answer the call which is of His creation?[16]

The final question is clearly the most theologically "risky" because it implies God is under compulsion to respond to prayer according to his will. But it is also extremely helpful because it makes the context interpersonal rather than mechanical (puppets), logical (paradox) or inhuman (monkeys). It also introduces the priority of love. I think Hammond is right; but you will have to make up your own mind.

Is there any biblical support? Just a little. In Isaiah 49:15 God says

to Israel:
> Can a mother forget the baby at her breast
>> and have no compassion on the child she has borne?
> Though she may forget,
>> I will not forget you!

And in Hosea 11:1-9 he says:
> When Israel was a child, I loved him,
>> and out of Egypt I called my son.
> But the more I called Israel,
>> the further they went from me.
> They sacrificed to the Baals
>> and they burned incense to images.
> It was I who taught Ephraim to walk,
>> taking them by the arms;
> but they did not realize
>> it was I who healed them.
> I led them with the cords of human kindness,
>> with ties of love;
> I lifted the yoke from their neck
>> and bent down to feed them. . . .
> My people are determined to turn from me.
>> Even if they call to the Most High,
>> he will by no means exalt them.
> How can I give you up, Ephraim?
>> How can I hand you over, Israel? . . .
> My heart is changed within me;
>> all my compassion is aroused.
> I will not carry out my fierce anger,
>> nor devastate Ephraim again.
> For I am God, and not man—
>> the Holy One among you.

In this text we first find that the love and care of God as parent is spelled out. Then we see the prayer of the rebellious child. God then hears the prayer, averts his anger and responds to the call of the child he nurtured. (One is tempted to point out especially the changing of God's heart in verse 8; but the Hebrew text here is not easily translated. RSV renders "My heart *recoils* within me"; the NKJV, "My heart *churns* within Me"; and the NASB, "My heart is *turned over* within Me.") God's response to the child's call, however, is unmistakable. It is the same with us. We are, as Israel was, God's children: "For he chose us in him before the creation of the world. . . . In love he predestined us to be adopted as his sons through Jesus Christ, in accordance with his pleasure and will" (Eph 1:4-5).

Why Don't I Get What I Pray For?

If I am God's child and he responds to my prayers, why do I not always get what I pray for? The standard reply here is to appeal to the inscrutable wisdom of God. Infinite Wisdom must often refuse what ignorance insists must be done. This makes sense logically, but theologically the best answer is found in 1 John 5:14-15: "If we ask anything according to his will, he hears us. And if we know that he hears us—whatever we ask—we know that we have what we asked of him."

Only prayer according to God's will is granted. Economically, this is the "bottom line"; and occasionally in their zeal to encourage faith, those who teach and write about prayer seem to forget it. We all want to be more "effective" in prayer—to see our petitions granted—but formulas and techniques which offer amazing results in inducing God to answer are purchased primarily by the spiritually immature.

During World War 2 *HIS* magazine ran a brief article by an army chaplain entitled "Some Pray and Die." This is still one of the most poignant statements in print about getting what you want through prayer. The chaplain asks:

Is there such a thing as getting the "breaks" in prayer? What about the fellows who pray regularly, but get killed regularly? . . . I wish people would stop writing about the soldiers who pray and have their prayers answered by *not* getting killed. Why do all the other soldiers seem to get the wrong answer?

What I want to know is this: what sort of an extra-special, super-powered prayer is needed to make everything turn out the way you want it? That sounds facetious, almost irreverent, but I'm serious. I really want to know. I'm an army chaplain, and I could use some special prayers with my men—and heaven knows, we need them badly at times. Because the fact is there are always more men who pray to come back than there are men who get back. Quite a lot more. What is the deciding factor?

The thing for all of us to remember is this: someone else does the answering. . . . What you have in mind may not be what God has in mind. If you ask him something, you must be willing to take what he gives. . . . That is why I am a bit depressed by the writings of those who try to get other people to pray by telling them that you get what you want. People must learn to want what they get. . . . When I talk to soldiers about prayer I try to tell them that they must be adults. God expects us to be men. Only children demand a happy ending to every story. How old must we be before we begin to realize that even prayer can't get us everything we want, unless the thing we want is right for us to have?

Who gets the breaks in prayers? Nobody. There is no such thing. We get what God in his infinite love and foreknowledge, sees fit to give. That's not always the same as getting what we want. But it ought to be.[17]

There are also certain practical problems involved with praying for what we want. Christians pray in conflict: for sun and for rain in the same town on the same day. We pray shortsightedly and often selfishly; our prayer desires are often more influenced by the immediate demands of our own situation and the culture around us than by longing for true justice. If I pray for you, my ignorance of what God knows you really need is sometimes appalling. On many days it is good that we don't get what we ask. And it is often arrogance, *not* great faith, which insists in prayer that God must respond in this way or that. An instance in Scripture which applies shows God sending people what *they* insisted was best so that they could learn what *he* knew was best. It is not a pretty picture:

But they soon forgot what he had done
and did not wait for his counsel.
In the desert they gave in to their craving;
in the wasteland they put God to the test.
So he gave them what they asked for,
but sent a wasting disease upon them. (Ps 106:13-15)

But there is little doubt that the major problem which would attach
to our getting 100% results in prayer is sin: vanity and pride. As C.
S. Lewis has said, "A man who knew empirically that an event had
been caused by his prayer would feel like a magician. His head
would turn and his heart would be corrupted."[18] I feel I am being
invited to plant seeds for this kind of rotten fruit whenever someone says that praying in a certain way will *guarantee* results. The
chaplain was right: "Only [selfish] children *demand* a happy ending
to every story" (or think the story ends tomorrow). True childlike
faith takes another approach: "*Abba*, Father, everything is possible
for you. Take this cup from me. Yet not what I will, but what you
will" (Mk 14:36).

Is "Thy Will Be Done" the Only Way to Pray?

I am not saying that Christians should merely lay out every situation before the Lord and say, "Thy will be done." This seems to be
done on occasion in Scripture (2 Kings 19:14-19; Acts 4:23-30). But
often prayer desires and God's will seem coherent. When this is so,
then we can pray with fervency and persistence. "Thy will be done"
is not a prayer formula but an *attitude*: a reflection of the petitioner's
willingness to admit that the Father's knowledge is more complete
than his children's. It expresses the child's wish to learn to want
what God gives. When the phrase seems appropriate use it. When
you don't, God sees the attitude it should represent.

The central practical issue of this chapter is represented by these
two verses:

Priority of my will: "We want you to do for us whatever we ask."
(Mk 10:35)

Priority of God's will: "If we ask anything according to his will, he hears us." (1 Jn 5:14)

God hears us (grants our petitions) *only* when we ask according to his will. "And how," you say, "can I know the will of God?" Here are some practical suggestions:

1. *Beware of the media.* It is safe to say that in general what is presented on the big silver screen, TV, radio and in print is designed to get you to see *your* will, not God's, as the most important thing there is. The appeal comes from the world and is directed toward human cravings. A steady diet of media metaphysics will slowly and surely seduce you to desire the transitory glitter of the world, not the imperishable glory of God. James points out the result: "When you ask, you do not receive, because you ask with wrong motives, that you may spend what you get on your pleasures" (4:3). Show biz is often not God's biz. As computer programmers say, "garbage in, garbage out." You must take charge of your life again: rescue your head from hedonism and hype. Go back to reading the Bible.

2. *Make Bible reading and study a priority.* Our Lord said, "If . . . my words remain in you, ask whatever you wish, and it will be given to you" (Jn 15:7). If you want to pray more effectively, do not ignore the revealed, written will of God in Scripture. No one expects a device to run if the operating instructions are not followed. Your prayer life is no different. Ignorance of spiritual principles does not make them of no effect—any more than your failure to notice a speed limit sign will make the traffic citation in your palm disappear. Petition, no matter how earnest, offered with wrong motives will *not* be answered. And prayer *can* be hindered by behavior which seems completely unrelated to your supplication (1 Pet 3:7). You don't need to become a professional Bible scholar to pray in God's will. But you must regularly read and begin to study the Scriptures.

3. *Commit yourself to doing God's will.* Basic Christian obedience is essential to praying according to God's will.

I urge you, brothers, in view of God's mercy, to offer your bodies as living sacrifices, holy and pleasing to God—which is your spiritual worship. Do not conform any longer to the pattern of this world, but be transformed by the renewing of your mind. *Then you will be able to test and approve what God's will* is—his good, pleasing and perfect will. (Rom 12:1-2)

4. *Remember you're a unique individual.* God's will for you is not necessarily the same as for your neighbor, brother, mother or best friend. Be careful not to determine God's will by looking at others. There are, of course, many good and positive models in the Christian community. But be open to let the Holy Spirit guide your thoughts, goals and prayer aspirations. Seek what God wills in and for your own life without making comparisons with others. It takes some effort to do this. Western society has institutionalized the "pecking order" as a way of life: constant evaluation to see who's better, or worse off, than I am. Avoid this like the plague.

5. *Learn from others, especially older Christians.* Seek the advice and guidance of others who were in the faith before you. Especially in the West, we are prone to relegate the gray head to the sewing circle and bowling outings. But as in most areas of life, experience counts a great deal. The one who can't play ball with you probably has more time to pray with and for you. The grandma who prays daily for five children and thirteen grandchildren may help you more with intercession than others who seem more spiritual on first impression. All the parts of the body of Christ need and can learn from the others. Praying in God's will is no exception.

6. *Pray for others and ask them to pray for you.* Make a specific contract with a friend to pray about something for a fixed period of time. When the period is up, check back with one another. Don't just say, "Pray for me," and ride off into the sunset. Be specific, make the commitment short enough to be reasonable, and ask for and provide feedback: "I'm worried about the way my relationship with Don is going, but I don't know how to pray about it. Will you ask God to help me know what to ask for? I'll call you Wednesday evening to talk." Paul wrote, "Since the day we heard about you, we have not stopped praying for you and asking God to fill you with the knowledge of his will through all spiritual wisdom and understanding" (Col 1:9).

No matter how large a spiritual giant you may become, there will be days when God's answer to your prayers will be no. Despite your seeking, searching and the outpouring of your soul, your heavenly Father has decided against your petition. When this happens your *attitude* becomes the vital factor. Are you willing to give your hurt, disappointment, perhaps even grief, to Christ who died for you . . . and then begin to pray again? Prayer problems are usually not intellectual, but volitional. In praying effectively the submission of your will is directly linked with finding God's will. Prayer which God answers is always offered with an attitude of submission.

Are you willing to say, when God's response to your urgent prayer is not the one you wanted: "Have thine own way, Lord"?

Questions for Thought and Discussion

1. Do you think answering a prayer for good weather is as complicated as the author suggests it is? Why do you answer as you do?

2. Do you tend to agree with S. D. Gordon or the author about the role of prayer and God's sovereignty? Does it matter how you look at it?

3. T. C. Hammond used kittens and monkeys to illustrate prayer and God's response. Try to come up with some other apt illustrations.

4. How did you react to the quotation by the chaplain in "Some Pray and Die"? Do you think it's childish to desire happy answers to prayer?

5. The happy—or dramatic—answers to prayer tend to get the most attention from fellow Christians and the Christian media. Does this help or hurt your attitude toward prayer?

6. Do you think it really matters whether Christians think about things like human freedom and God's sovereignty when they pray? Why or why not?

7. At the chapter's end the author claims that "prayer problems are usually not intellectual, but volitional." What do you think he means by this? Can you think of evidence which would support or disallow this idea?

5
Spirit:
How Do I Speak to
an Invisible God?

Billy, alone and frightened in his dark bedroom, called to his mother. She quickly responded to his voice: "Don't be afraid, Billy. God is always with us, even though we can't see him."

"It would help a lot more," said Billy, "if there was a *real* person here with skin on."

I feel like Billy every time I pray. God is Spirit, we are told (Jn 4:24), and he lives in unapproachable light. No one has ever seen or can see him (1 Tim 6:16). Since a spirit does not have flesh and bones, God by nature does not have any skin on (Lk 24:39). Yet all the real people I talk to daily do. Even the disembodied words which come to me from the telephone, radio or tape recorder are the voices of people with skin on. And the computer-synthesized utterance which calls me a "chicken" when I play a video game was programmed into the machine by someone I could see. But God is different. He is invisible. And this invisibility affects people in different ways.

Talking to the God You Can't See

First, when we can't see something it remains abstract. Some process of visualization (if only mental) usually precedes understanding. That's why "one picture is worth a thousand words." Since we can't see God, it becomes easy to think of him as an abstraction, a divine Something we are told exists, but which is not really comprehensible. Calling God "the Great Spirit," "the Power of the Universe," "the Wholly Other" or "the Force" may result from this. You may stand in awe of such a deified cosmic flux—as many do of electricity—but you can't talk with it as you might a *real* person.

Second, since God as Spirit is invisible, he may become an object of fear. Things which are not visible can seem unintelligible, and what we don't understand we often fear. The converse is that persons who do see (or think they see) spirits usually get scared. Certainly this is true in Scripture. And the case with respect to God is well founded: "No one may see me and live" (Ex 33:20). Not only is there potential to fear this invisible Spirit, but nearly all who thought they saw him were terrorized by the experience. God's spirituality can produce anxiety which works against prayer.

Third, to make it seem reasonable to talk with an invisible God, most of us conceive of him as a person—perhaps bigger or more dignified and often much older, but generally like other human beings. Yet we will sometimes visualize God in a way which denies his true "otherness." We may remove the essence of his divinity and "see" an overly humanized One who is merely a reflection of our experience and desires. This can facilitate prayer, but are we speaking with God or to a figure from our own imaginations?

Fourth, we pray to the God we can't see in the company of people we can see. Naturally we are concerned about what impression our prayer is making on those people. So we tend to pray to the group which is visible rather than to God who is invisible. We are also prone to focus on how our words might impress God *if* he were like those we are praying with. And even when praying alone we wonder, Do I sound sincere? Is he getting the point that I'm in a really desperate situation? I wonder if it would help if I got down on my knees. Each of us struggles to reconcile truths like "God is Spirit" with the more tangible material of daily life.

God's Personhood

The Bible does say, "God is Spirit." But Scripture does not teach that God is pure abstract Spirit, but rather *personal* Spirit. For example, God has a personal name. Spelled with the Hebrew consonants *YHWH*, this name is vocalized by academics as "Yahweh," "Yahveh" or "Yahoveh." It is commonly pronounced "Jehovah." *YHWH* is an expression of God's eternality and his active presence among and concern for his people (Ex 3:14-15; 20:2). God's name is far more common in the Bible than we realize, because translators use the more formal expressions *Lord* and *God* in its place. (The New American Standard Bible, for instance, renders *YHWH* as *God* 315 times, *Lord* 6,399 times and *Lord's* 111 times. A similar pattern is found in nearly all versions.) Yet the terms *Lord* and *God* are impersonal, almost by definition, and carry little of the relational dynamic which undergirds personal prayer in Scripture. If I said God's personal name was Bob, you might think the idea was blasphemous. Bob means something to you because you know someone (or about someone) with that name, and it brings up various images about Bob's character, personality and activities. Somehow it does not seem right to know the Lord God as you know Bob, yet it appears that is precisely why God revealed his name to us. He did it so that his people might think of him as a living, divine Person with whom relationship was possible. Jehovah is not a dead idol or a cosmic it.

Scripture makes it clear that God is self-conscious and able to determine the course of his life. He does this on the basis of the rational exercise of an individual intelligence. He has a will and is able to act, to do things such as search, reveal and create. Further, he does them in a way that demonstrates moral character. He also possesses pure emotions such as love and righteous anger. He knows both grief and joy. The Bible describes him (in both testaments) as a Father who has children with whom he desires to share himself in personal relationship, fellowship and mutual self-disclosure. All these things constitute what it means to be personal.

Yet some people object to calling God personal. The Bible never actually applies the term *person* to God. And the idea of personhood can, if taken too far, demean the dignity of God's divinity. Since the word *person* is usually applied to created human beings rather than to their Creator, it might be better to say that there is personality *in* God, or something similar. Yet surely the anthropomorphic and anthropopathic language which Scripture applies to God indicates some analogy between the human being and the Supreme Being. Where does the so-called personalness which characterizes us come from? Not from the warm molecular soup from which many claim we emerged, but rather from our personal Creator himself. Human personhood is an aspect of what it means to be made in God's image and likeness. It reflects the interpersonal love and communication which have eternally characterized the Godhead—Father, Son and Holy Spirit.

However, God gave the final word on his divine personhood himself. Aware of the inherent limitations of our humanness when thinking about his nature as Spirit, God chose not to remain eternally invisible. He put "skin on" and showed us what he is like in the person of the Lord Jesus. So the apostle John understood it: "The Word became flesh and lived for a while among us" (Jn 1:14); "No man has seen God at any time; [but] the only begotten God who is in the bosom of the Father, He has explained Him" (Jn 1:18 NASB); "Anyone who has seen me has seen the Father" (Jn 14:9). So that we might be sure the personal representation of God in Jesus is accurate, Paul adds, "He is the image of the invisible God. . . . God was pleased to have all his fullness dwell in him" (Col 1:15, 19). Thus, the writer to the Hebrews confirms this: "The Son is the radiance of God's glory and the exact representation of his being" (1:3). If you spend just thirty minutes reading one of the Gospels, you cannot fail to see that the writer—whether Matthew, Mark, Luke or John—wants you to believe that Jesus (and hence his eternal God and Father) was fully personal.

The fact of God's personalness means that knowing *about* him is different than knowing him. Most of what the Bible says about prayer assumes this distinction. But we forget this. We tend to view prayer as a process of gathering information about God and practicing certain techniques. But prayer is interpersonal communication between two individuals. In Scripture it matters far, far less *how, when* and *what* you say than how well you know *him* to whom you pray. Many of the Bible's instructions about prayer make more sense when looked at in the context of God's personalness. I'd like to look at some of those instructions in the rest of this chapter and offer practical suggestions on the mechanics of prayer.

Praying to a Personal God
In that part of Matthew's Gospel known as the Sermon on the Mount, the Lord said:

Be careful not to do your "acts of righteousness" before men, to be seen by them. If you do, you will have no reward from your Father in heaven. . . .

When you pray, do not be like the hypocrites, for they love to pray standing in the synagogues and on the street corners to be seen by men. I tell you the truth, they have received their reward in full. (Mt 6:1, 5)

Jesus envisions a person who offers prayers in public in order that others might see (and hear) and call him righteous. (Perhaps it is the practice described in Luke 20:47 as "for a show make lengthy prayers.") Jesus' words seem like a straightforward warning about acting spiritual to impress others. We might also see them as an admonition that acts of piety should grow out of the right motives. But Jesus' words are primarily a statement that God, like all personal beings, dislikes being *used* by others in pursuit of objectives which are personally offensive to him. God is not merely a Something to be exploited while passing on to some other goal; rather he is Somebody, a person who reacts against having his name used in self-aggrandizement. Hypocrisy *per se* is not Jesus' objection. Being a religious actor is an external symptom of a more serious internal malady: depersonalized thinking about the nature of God.

The whole of Matthew 6 could be boiled down to a statement that our personal God does not care to be treated as a nonperson: as if it didn't matter whether he was there at all. Naturally, he does not encourage his own depersonalization by "rewarding" this kind of prayer. In fact, such words are not really prayer directed to him at all; they are spoken to another audience. The reward for such prayer is flattery.[1] God's goal in prayer, which is satisfying communion and growth in our understanding of him, is totally lost. Given this perspective, what Jesus says in the next verse follows naturally.

Time Alone with God
"When you pray, go into your room, close the door and pray to your Father, who is unseen. Then your Father, who sees what is done in secret, will reward you" (Mt 6:6).

Jesus gives this instruction because we all desire the approval of others, and the seed from which hypocrisy blooms is well rooted in each of us. But the more significant point is that it takes time alone, away from the pressures of life in general and the expectations of others in particular, before two persons are likely to come to know and genuinely understand each other. As a relationship grows, it is natural to want to talk alone. Do you know any lovers who want to spend all their time in the presence of others? Praying with others or leading others in group prayer is not wrong, as Jesus' own attendance at the synagogue demonstrates. Nor is it inherently wrong to offer personal prayer in front of others as all Jesus' prayers in John's Gospel show us (see Lk 4:16; Jn 6:11; 11:41-42; 12:27-28 and 17). But such activities are *not* a substitute for time alone with God.

The nature of personality is such that we are rarely able to bare ourselves in public, and often it would be inappropriate to do so. But in God we have one—maybe the only one some days—who because he loves us has *only* our best interest at heart. Who else could we trust with the very core of our beings? As James said, "Come near to God and he will come near to you" (Jas 4:8).[2]

Here then is a biblical basis for having a "quiet time" alone with the Lord. The practice of daily personal devotions has been characteristic of spiritually sincere people for centuries. It is said of Daniel, for example, "Three times a day he got down on his knees and prayed, giving thanks to his God" (Dan 6:10). Though this was a custom among pious Jews in his day, Daniel's private prayer life apparently didn't become perfunctory. But it is easy for such a habit to become spiritually sterile. An encouraging environment and routine are helpful to many, but when the time, place or pattern of activity becomes critical, then form has replaced function. Where there is a stable, maturing relationship with God, the occasional absence of opportunity for time alone with him should not "just ruin my entire day." Jesus desired that we go into our room and close the door and pray so as to know and learn to depend on God himself, not the elements which constitute the quiet time. Yet the importance of finding time to pray alone cannot be overstressed. Through the gradual building of a relationship with God, gained during periodic times alone, we lay the foundation of interpersonal stability with him which allows us to come in times of crisis and triumph and find the strength to keep life in perspective . . . his perspective.[3]

To Get Up or Not

Christians are sometimes told they should rise by at least 6:00 A.M. every morning to pray for thirty minutes. "Jesus got up early to pray and you should be doing it too," we are told. And historical precedent may be used for more clout: "Whenever Martin Luther knew he was going to have a tough day he got up *another* hour earlier so he could pray longer." Now if you have not been having early morning prayer, all this may depress rather than inspire you.

My encouragement would be to mention that Martin Luther also went to bed about as early as his chickens, and to observe that Jesus also prayed throughout the day, evening and night hours.[4] Our Lord does not come on the air for prayer only between 6:00 and 6:30. Pray when it best fits your schedule. Pick a time you can look forward to rather than dread. Start by praying for as long as you are comfortable. This will probably be longer than you thought, but if it means only five minutes a day, then do it.

And don't feel guilty because you are not yet a great prayer warrior. Warriors are trained; and training takes both time and experience. Luther went through years of structured spiritual training and monastic experience before he developed the prayer habits one so often hears about.[5] Your desire to pray will grow. Those who taste find that the Lord is good. Some day you may find prayer so invigorating that you will agree with the psalmist: "As the deer pants for the water brooks, so my soul pants for Thee, O God. My soul thirsts for God, for the living God" (Ps 42:1-2 NASB).

Remember also that God, like the rest of us, finds it somewhat less than captivating when you fall asleep on him while talking. Paul seemed to be aiming at this when he urged: "Devote yourselves to prayer, keeping *alert* in it" (Col 4:2 NASB). And Peter adds: "Be *clearminded* and self-controlled so that you can pray" (1 Pet 4:7). To communicate effectively you have to think; and to make sense you have to be organized. It is not otherwise with God.

Praying out loud—even though alone—helps some, while using notes, lists and prayer notebooks may help organization and memory. Some find fasting helps their mental acuity, and so they eat after they pray. Those with lower blood sugar levels must eat before they pray. Some people pray in their night clothes while others are fully dressed. If obeying Paul's admonition to "sing . . . with gratitude in your hearts to God" (Col 3:16) is easiest when you're undergoing the stimulation of a shower, then praise him in the privacy of your bathroom.

The point is to look for the most helpful time of day, find out what will help you get focused and *do* it.

"But I Just Don't Know What to Say"

Feeling inadequate as you approach prayer is a common experience. If you've been asked to lead others in public worship, ask a friend for help or get some ideas from the Psalms. Use notes or an outline to pray from. Make no apology for doing so. There is nothing wrong with reading a prayer, even another's prayer if you can make it your own. If there were, God would not have to put so many prayers in Scripture. Use ordinary language which can be understood by those you have been asked to lead. Feel no guilt if you can't pronounce sufficient Elizabethan English to sound "spiritual." The biblical languages were not sixteenth-century English. They were the tongues of ordinary life: the kind of speech heard in the markets, on fishing boats and at family suppers. Scripture uses no special "spiritual" vocabulary. Greek-speaking Christians in the New Testament era were not required to pray in Hebrew or Aramaic, the languages and idiom of another time, land and culture.

Look over the example of prayer Jesus gave in Matthew 6:9-13 and Luke 11:2-4. Notice the brevity and simplicity of the Lord's Prayer. Pray to God in public with courtesy and respect.[6] Words of reverence, honor and esteem are always appropriate, but avoid ostentation and ponderousness like the plague. *Be yourself.* After all, they've asked *you* to pray, not somebody else.

If you are *praying alone,* it is still all right to use notes or to read your prayers. Spontaneous prayer does not come easily for everybody, and it is doubtful that extemporaneous hodgepodge is any more authentic than a written meditation. If it is one of those days when nothing comes, then tell God, "I want to be alone with you, but I can't think of anything to say." Or open your Bible and read one of David's prayers in the Psalms. Maybe his words will help you find yours. God knows what your day has been like, where your physiology is, where your emotions have been and how much is ahead for you yet. People who love each other don't *have* to talk all the time they are together.[7] (In fact, incessant chatter may be a sign of insecurity in relationships.) If when you do eventually begin to pray you trip on your thoughts or tongue, don't worry about it. God is the only one to whom you can say, "You know what I mean," and be 100% sure you will not be misunderstood.

At the height of his spiritual maturity Paul acknowledged, "we do not know what we ought to pray." But he went immediately on to say, "the Spirit himself intercedes for us with groans that words cannot express. . . . The Spirit intercedes for the saints in accordance with God's will" (Rom 8:26-27). Jesus himself once prayed, "Now, my heart is troubled, and what shall I say?" (Jn 12:27). Now Jesus is closer to God than any other, "at the right hand of God . . . interceding for us" (Rom 8:34). Through the intercession of Jesus and the Spirit, God has provided for our inadequacies.

"How Will I Know When God Speaks to Me?"

This question is not usually mentoned in books on prayer. It has no simple answer. God has spoken to people in many different ways, and those who write books on prayer must not either limit or predict how God may communicate with you. God spoke audibly to Moses (Ex 3:4-5), Samuel (1 Sam 3:1-2) and Elijah (1 Kings 19:13-14). And a few Christians in our time also say they have heard his voice. Some say they have heard God's voice "inside" (inaudibly) during prayer. God has also responded to prayer by "speaking" during dreams (Acts 16:9). Some have been visited by angels with God's response to prayer (Dan 9:20-23; Acts 27:23), and others have experienced visions (Acts 9:11-15; 10:2-7). In some cases the response of the Lord was given to a third party who then told the petitioner (2 Kings 20:2-7; Acts 9:10). Occasionally an angel has been sent to a third party in response to prayer (Acts 12:5-11).

Nevertheless, most Christians in our day do not routinely experience these types of responses to their prayers. Many never do. Because this is true, we need guidelines to test the responses.

"How do I know," Ebenezer Scrooge asked the specter of Christmas past in Dickens's *A Christmas Carol*, "that you are not just a blot of mustard or a fragment of an underdone potato?" This is a relevant question. Be honest, and evaluate your physical, emotional and mental state when any word from the Lord is received. A dream produced by indigestion is likely not an inspiration from God. More importantly, evaluate the content of God's apparent response against the content of his certain Word. No reply of God's to prayer will ever conflict with Scripture. If you need help, seek the wisdom and advice of your pastor or elders. If the message causes red flags to wave when explained to others in the body of Christ, evaluate carefully and proceed slowly. Take no precipitous action. People arrested every year with bombs and guns say, "God told me to do it."

Generally God's response to prayer is not extraordinary. Prayer is not an invitation to a side show. For the few who have audibly heard God's voice or seen his angel, there are thousands more who discern his response in very ordinary ways.

God's reply to prayer may come during your time of devotion. You may find yourself remembering a part of Scripture which directly applies to your petition or which states a general principle which covers the concern at hand. But for this to happen you must *first* have read, if not actually memorized, sufficient Scripture for the Spirit to have something to bring to mind. God speaks through his Word frequently. Some come away from prayer convicted that a course of action is the one God desires them to take, or certain that another is wrong. The petitioner becomes convinced the action is consistent with general biblical guidelines. After prayer, God's answer may be discerned through private Bible reading or study with a friend. Maybe he will be heard in the words of your pastor, an elder or Sunday-school teacher. Perhaps it will be during dialog with a counselor or friend. After he called on the name of the Lord, Abraham once received a stinging rebuke, clearly an admonition from God, from an abject pagan (Gen 20:1-18).

Christians often say they received no answer concerning a matter prayed about, but God gave them "peace" about it. Having peace after prayer is the way some believers gain assurance that their petitions are heard. But *peace* is a much misused word. If you have peace that God will do what you could but don't want to do, a more accurate word might be *fear* or *laziness*. If peace means you have not really given the situation much thought, but just passed it on to God, then perhaps *irresponsible* is closer to the truth. If peace means you did not talk the problem over with another believer, maybe *introverted* or *pig-headed* applies. Obviously I feel uncomfortable about finding God's will only through feelings called "peace."

God also responds to prayer by changing circumstances. In such cases God's response takes more the form of doing than directing, convicting or giving peace. But there are obviously times when God does not change circumstances. When this happens, it can be difficult to know how to judge the situation. If the opportunity has passed, then God's answer is likely to be no. If God still could act in the future, we then wonder whether to keep on praying or not. Here the presence or absence of what was called peace seems important.

Convinced that he should go to Rome, Paul prayed a long time for God to arrange it. But he was hindered, his plans constantly thwarted (Rom 1:10-13). Yet he persisted in prayer. The desire to go was apparently not removed, and he received no impression that he could not go. Further, he asked Roman Christians to join him in praying "that by God's will I may come to you with joy" (Rom 15:31-32). He received God's assurance weeks later while imprisoned in Jerusalem (Acts 23:11) but was not told how this would be accomplished. It would take more than two years of imprisonment in Caesarea before he set sail—still a prisoner—for Italy. Paul was again given divine encouragement that he would eventually get to Rome (Acts 27:23), but this was followed by a storm which raged for two weeks, a shipwreck and consequent three-month delay on an island due to winter gales. God's final answer was perhaps two and a half years in coming. The story is a monument to persistence in prayer.

Elsewhere Paul relates an attempt by repeated pleading prayer to get God to remove a physical discomfort or infirmity (2 Cor 12:7-10). God replied that he would not remove the weakness. One gets the impression that Paul did not pray about it any longer. This time he apparently had peace and found God's grace sufficient for his suffering. Once, Moses was actually forbidden to pray any longer for God to reverse his judgment and let him enter Canaan. "That is enough," the LORD said. "Do not speak to me anymore about this matter" (Deut 3:26; see also Jer 7:16). It is hard to say that Moses had peace about the situation, but he knew he was to stop praying.

If the opportunity for God to act is not gone and he has not told you to stop praying, I would encourage you to persist. Your attitude should parallel David's, "Who knows? The LORD may be gracious to me" (2 Sam 12:22). But don't persist to wear God down as if he were a disinterested mechanical deity (Mt 6:7), a reluctant and inconvenienced friend (Lk 11:5-7) or a corrupt but harassed judge (Lk 18:1-6). Be importunate because you as God's children are *completely dependent* on your loving heavenly Father for that which is petitioned: "Whom have I in heaven but you?" (Ps 73:25). Reflecting on the reality of God's personalness keeps importunity and persistence from becoming mechanical techniques for manipulation.

God's personalness may also explain why answers to prayer are not always immediately given. Most of us tend to view getting answers as the *goal* and prayer as the *means* to that end. But God views it differently. Given the perfection of his person, it is certain that God does not *need* us to talk to him because he's lonely or insecure, nor does he have to depend on our advice or help in running the universe. Yet the commands in Scripture to pray suggest that he *wants* us to pray; he actually enjoys having us speak to him. Developing a relationship with us is God's goal, and answers to prayer are a means he uses to foster self-disclosure, growth and understanding of both him and ourselves.

Since we are given to longer petitions than thanksgivings, it may be that for God to answer our prayers immediately might help depersonalize our thinking about him and be counterproductive to growth in our relationship with him. Let me illustrate. My son, Doug, spoke with me for many hours over several months about the advantages of the frame, chain, brakes and shifters found on a certain ten-speed bike he hoped to own. When Doug got such a vehicle, he spent far more time riding it and showing it to his friends than talking to me about it. If I had purchased it for him the day after he first mentioned it, the whole process—during which we learned far more about each other than about the bike Doug wanted—would have been cut to less than five minutes.

God may ask you to wait for answers to prayer not only because he loves you and knows what is best, but also because he actually *likes* you as an individual and *personally enjoys* having you talk to him.

"But What If God Does Not Respond at All?"

What should we do when God does not seem to answer our prayers? I would encourage you to pray and then exercise your God-given intellect. Examine the situation in light of Scripture and common knowledge, seek the advice and counsel of other believers, evaluate your skills, abilities and gifts, and consider the impact the alternatives will have on yourself and others. Review the factors involved with the Lord in prayer, ask for his help and then make a decision. Trust the Lord to direct your steps. With his Word in your mind, his Spirit in your heart and a desire to please him impressed on your will, you may follow what seems the best course and assume that such a course is God's answer to prayer. "In his heart a man plans his course, but the LORD determines his steps" is the way this idea is expressed in Proverbs 16:9. Perhaps God's answer to your prayer may be: "What do *you* think? And when are you going to do something about it?"

Far too many Christians use prayer as a sanctified excuse for procrastination and passivity. The fact is most of us would rather pray about it than do something about it. We must be willing to both pray *and* act. *Personal responsibility* characterized Jesus' relationship with God. We need to follow his example by giving responsible service to God, even as we ask him to give to us in prayer. And we must not expect God to do for us what he has given us the ability to do for ourselves. "If you loved me, you would help," we want to pray. But he replies in the silence, "Because I love you, I won't. I'll help you to do it yourself."

Understanding God's existence as personal spirit undergirds almost everything else which might be said about prayer. God's personalness is the factor which makes prayer voluntary interpersonal communication and communion rather than compulsory mechanical manipulation and exploitation. Not until we come to view God *himself* as our treasure in heaven are we likely to genuinely *desire* to pray. "For where your treasure is, there your heart will be also" (Mt 6:21).

Questions for Thought and Discussion

1. Do you think it is right to say that God is a person? Explain.

2. What can we do to avoid praying to other people rather than to God at prayer meetings? How can you help another person feel comfortable praying out loud at such meetings?

3. Do you like to pray? Why or why not? Do you think God likes to have you pray? Explain why you feel that way.

4. Do you think it is right biblically to say that prayer should be viewed primarily as a way to build a relationship with God rather than a way to get answers? Why is it hard to remember that when God does not answer your prayer?

5. What practical suggestions have helped you most in your prayer life? Why?

6. What do you think about the author's ideas concerning having peace after you pray?

6
Good:
Why Pray to One Who
Lets People Hurt?

Mary, who loved Christ and lived life larger than even pulp-fiction authors usually conceive, died in her early twenties of rampaging carcinoma . . . the same summer she was going to teach my son to swim. And Bill, among the brightest called to Gospel ministry, stopped breathing on a table in his doctor's office. He was in class taking notes on Bible interpretation one day . . . leaving a widow and tiny infant the next. Then there was the young, all-American accountant at my church. Greg kissed his wife and little daughter and took his Bible along to Reserve training . . . and flew his jet fighter into a forest.

Seminary professors are supposed to have answers to such traumas. I talked about God's will with Mary for hours following her

surgery, but with Bill's young wife for only a few embarrassed
moments. As I prepared the message for the funeral of the Marine
Corps pilot, the Scripture that kept coming to mind was this:

Why do the wicked live on,
    growing old and increasing in power?
They see their children established around them,
    their offspring before their eyes.
They send forth their children as a flock;
    their little ones dance about.
They sing to the music of the tambourine and harp;
    they make merry to the sound of the flute.
They spend their years in prosperity
    and go down to the grave in peace.
Yet they say to God, "Leave us alone!
    We have no desire to know your ways.
Who is the Almighty, that we should serve him?
    What would we gain by praying to him?" (Job 21:7-8, 11-15)

All I felt I could pray to God was "Why?" And God, for his part,
said nothing . . . nothing at all.

The Silence of God

This sort of experience is only part of what theologians call the
silence of God. Describing it Arthur Custance says,

It is His seeming indifference, at times, to the needs of human
beings when appalling suffering overtakes them. Countless millions of people have suffered because of famine or war or
drought or disaster in circumstances in which it hardly seems
appropriate to say they *deserved* it.

At such times thoughtful men do not become atheists because
they find it irrational to believe in a spiritual world which is
above and beyond demonstration by ordinary means, but because of emotional insult, the feeling that if God is really such
a Being as we, his children, claim Him to be, He could not pos-
sibly remain silent. He would have to act manifestly, mercifully,
savingly, publicly.[1]

The end of these three promising young lives was jarring to me. The tragedy of their apparently senseless and purposeless deaths has become for me a reminder of what Sir Robert Anderson so emotively described almost a century ago:

Society, even in the great centres of our modern civilisation, is all too like a slave-ship, where, with the sounds of music and laughter and revelry on the upper deck, there mingle the groans of untold misery battened down below. Who can estimate the sorrow and suffering and wrong endured during a single round of the clock?

From the old days of Pagan Rome right down through the centuries of so-called "Christian" persecutions, the untold millions of the martyrs, the best and purest of our race have been given up to violence and outrage and death in hideous forms. The heart grows sick at the appalling story, and we turn away with a dull but baseless hope that it may be in part at least untrue. But the facts are too terrible to make exaggeration in the record of them possible. Torn by wild beasts in the arena, torn by men as merciless as wild beasts, and, far more hateful, in the torture chambers of the Inquisition, His people have died, with faces turned to heaven, and hearts upraised in prayer to God; but the heaven has seemed as hard as brass, and the God of their prayers as powerless as themselves or as callous as their persecutors![2]

The silence of a wise and good God is shattering.

Where Is God When It Hurts?

No thinking Christian will be able to evade the issue of God's silence and inactivity in the face of suffering. On some days we may find prayer impossible. Pain, anguish and grief can become so consuming that there is nothing left over to pray with. There *are* periods when the emotional insult of evil, injustice and destruction leave us emotionally, intellectually and spiritually numb.[3]

Actually, the desire to pray to God can make the problem worse. Precisely because there is supposed to be a wise and good God to pray to—because the Christian is *not* an atheist—he or she finds a conflict which makes the times of God's silence even more numbing. The big question is, why does pain and suffering exist? And given their existence, how do I respond to God in prayer?

Life once was good all the time. But God's creatures, both angelic and human, were created with the ability and freedom to enjoy and glorify him, or to rebel and sin against him. Satan and his demons chose to rebel. And as both biblical and secular history show . . . so did men and women. The result of this rebellion has been pain and hurt.

In an ultimate sense, our experience of both so-called natural and moral evil has its origin in rebellion against God (Gen 3:17-19). God chose to create beings in his image, capable of making responsible decisions rather than controlled by instinct (as animals) or electromechanical design (as machines). At its heart, our question comes down to a statement that pain and hurt exist in our world because beings like ourselves exist. The ability to love carries with it the ability to hurt. And the ability to glorify God carries the ability to sin. Our creaturely freedom makes possible agony, tyranny and oppression.

We must, as the title of Theodore Plantinga's helpful book suggests, set our minds to *Learning to Live with Evil.*[4] We *are* the children of Adam and Eve and must live in a world devastated by sin and evil. Speculation about what life would be like if we couldn't sin, like most theological speculation, helps us cope with life not one whit.

God Makes Evil into Good

Some Christians believe that God always turns evil into good. Alvera Mickelsen deals with this question, relating it to the death of John the Baptist:

There is no clue as to why God permitted John to be beheaded in a silly display of power by Herod. So far as we know, Jesus did not tell his disciples either that a great good would result from it, or that they should "praise the Lord" for the tragedy. He just went away alone to mourn John's death. . . .

To assume that God lets bad things happen so that we can experience greater good is to deny the basic reality of sin and its evil nature. Christ gave his life to deliver us from the ultimate penalty of sin and moral evil. When we say that good will always be the ultimate outcome of any "bad" happening, we are saying that moral evil does not really exist—it only seems that way to our mortal minds.

When an innocent child (or John the Baptist) is murdered, that is *evil*. Yes, God can, and often does, bring good results (conversions, family reconciliations, and so on) from such horrible events. But no parent would choose to let his child be cruelly murdered *so that* these "good things" would result. Friends who have faced tragic losses are not usually comforted by well-meaning friends who tell them "someday you will understand God's reasons."[5]
The facts are that God does not make evil into good. Evil remains evil no matter how much good God may eventually be pleased to reveal.

Romans 8:28 does not say that God makes all things good, but rather that "in all things God works for the good of those who love him." Confidence in God's love, presence and providence does not require that we deny the objective reality of evil or say that pain really does not hurt. Jesus delighted in doing God's will, but he did not delight to go to the cross. The text says that Jesus "for the joy set before him *endured* the cross" (Heb 12:2). Any five-year-old child knows that you *endure* spinach, rutabaga and liver. Strawberry shortcake, chocolate ice cream and other good things are not endured— they are enjoyed. Given his omniscient knowledge of the plan of salvation as God's eternal Son, Jesus saw joy before him, but as a man he did not enjoy either the prospect of, or the eventual reality of, the cross.

There is too much agony in Gethsemane to believe the Savior was "just praising the Lord" on the Mount of Olives. Luke 22:44 says he was in anguish and sweat profusely. Hebrews 5:7 says he cried. He asked for the help of friends who failed him (Mk 14:32), and he needed the help of an angel to continue (Lk 22:43). If our Lord and Master could be deeply distressed and troubled in the face of sin and evil, if he could say, "My soul is overwhelmed with sorrow to the point of death" (Mk 14:33-34), if he could cry . . . then why is it that we Christians continue to pretend—in the name of living the abundant or victorious life—that somehow it is good for bad things to happen and that dark is really light from God's point of view?[6]

If Jesus recoiled in abhorrence from personal suffering, by what sleight of hand do we conclude that it is "spiritual" to put on a happy face and lie to one another saying things like, "someday we'll understand; . . . these things always work out for good"? Do promises that "I shall know fully, even as I am fully known" (1 Cor 13:12) mean that Christians will become omniscient? Certainly not.[7] Because he was divine as well as human, Jesus understood the purpose of his suffering. But those who are only human are required to experience hurt, pain and suffering (even vicariously when others are in anguish) *without* certain knowledge about God's purpose in causing or permitting it.

It is nevertheless reasonable, given what is revealed about God's nature in Scripture, to *assume* that God does not permit or cause suffering in a believer's life as an end in itself. And despite our inner feelings that "we" or "they" don't deserve to suffer, we must be open to the possibility that God intends for us to respond to suffering with questions about *our* holiness and justice, rather than about his. In his book *Encourage Me: Caring Words for Heavy Hearts* Chuck Swindoll says,

> Crisis crushes. And in crushing, it often refines and purifies. You may be discouraged today because the crushing has not led to a surrender. I've stood beside too many of the dying, ministered to too many of the broken and bruised to believe that crushing is an end in itself. Unfortunately, however, it usually takes the brutal blows of affliction to soften and penetrate hard hearts. Even though such blows seem unfair.[8]

Swindoll goes on to quote Alexandr Solzhenitsyn's statement about his own suffering:

It was only when I lay there on rotting prison straw that I sensed within myself the stirrings of good. Gradually, it was disclosed to me that the line separating good and evil passes, not through states, nor between classes, nor between political parties either, but right through all human hearts. So, bless you, prison, for having been in my life.[9]

So What's This Got to Do with Prayer?

I do not think we Christians can begin to pray effectively for ourselves or others in pain until we are honest. Because of our creatureliness, much, if not most, human suffering seems meaningless. Our conjectures about why people hurt obscure the fact that *we simply don't know why*. It may seem helpful to suppose that God is doing or will do something good in these circumstances. But the truth is that we, like Job and the mothers of Bethlehem, usually don't know what is going on. What we know is that it hurts.

What we must stop doing is trying to be God, who *can* figure things out, and admit that we are creatures who cry. There is no victory in that (pagan) stoicism which says, "Smile even though it hurts; remember your testimony." Such attitudes are a victory for deception and spiritual schizophrenia. Wonder Woman and Superman exist only in fantasy. And Christians who believe they must thank God for hurt are masochists who make God into a sadist.[10] Read the Psalms again. Notice how honest David is when he prays, admitting his anguish, sorrow, grief and affliction (Ps 31:7, 9-10). We need not pretend to enjoy pain and anguish in order to be found faithful and pray effectively.

The desire to be victorious in adversity can create divisions among Christians. Many of us wish to be victorious enough not to need the support and help of others. Not that we are unwilling to pray for and assist others—all victorious Christians do that. Rather, we have a feeling that it is wrong to find ourselves in the position of having to depend on others and their intercession. Part of the reason why we find it hard to be helpful to someone in agony is that

we realize it could happen to us. And our desire to be independent—
to be omnipotent and need nobody else—is threatened. Hurt and
pain bring us back to the reality of our creatureliness and dependency. *We need other people.* It is sin, vanity and godless egoism, not
the principles of victorious Christian living, which have convinced
us otherwise.

Truly victorious Christians are those who admit their humanness
and who admit the emotional insult of God's apparent silence when
we suffer. They submit themselves to others and their Creator
with tears on their faces. Such Christians can pray like Jesus, "Not
as I will, but as thou wilt." Jesus was heard, we are told in Hebrews
5:7, because of his "godly fear" (RSV) or "reverent submission"
(NIV). He was not heard because he whistled in the dark. Jesus'
words showed his unconditional trust *in the midst* of fear and pain.[11]
In his *Psalms of My Life,* Joseph Bayly writes this prayer:

I cry tears
to you Lord
tears
because I cannot speak.
Words are lost
among my fears
pain
sorrows
losses
hurts
but tears
You understand
my wordless prayer
You hear.
Lord
wipe away my tears
all tears
not in distant day
but now
here.[12]

When we stop pretending with ourselves, one another and with our Lord, this is the sort of prayer which comes forth.

Where the Buck Finally Stops

We will begin to reconstruct our prayer life during and after suffering by letting go of the why questions. We should ask instead, as Philip Yancey does, Where is God when it hurts?[13] The answer to this question is certain: He is on the cross, taking to himself in Christ the pain, agony and terror of all the suffering in the whole universe. "God was in Christ reconciling the world to Himself" (2 Cor 5:19 NASB). "He is the atoning sacrifice for our sins, and not only for ours but also for the sins of the whole world" (1 Jn 2:2). As Hugh Silvester says:

God has "underwritten" and carried to Himself the incalculable suffering of the whole universe. The spectacle of Him merely sitting above the earth, "arranging" things, watching with detached interest the suffering of His creatures, measuring that suffering with delicate cosmic galvanometers and comparing it with equally sensitive readings on the good side . . . is indeed revolting. But I do not find this picture of God in the Bible. . . . One thing seems to me self-evident: that every particle of suffering in the whole belongs to Him as subject. He underwrote the whole cost Himself. Every time a rabbit is pursued, or a widow cries, or a man acts like a beast, God is there bearing it all. . . . God is "responsible" for all the suffering because He is Creator. As Redeemer He has carried that responsibility.[14]

It may not seem obvious that on the cross Jesus entered into suffering for nonbelievers and animals, but what seems unmistakable is that God directly identifies with Christian suffering. Christ himself asked the violent Saul, "Why do you persecute *me?*" (Acts 9:4). And we can draw a similar implication from Matthew where Jesus says, "Whatever you did for one . . . of these brothers of mine, you did for me" (25:40). God does not watch us suffer from the security of a painless heaven, where all is bliss and joy. In Jesus he *is* a man of sorrows, acquainted with grief. Our question *How can we pray to a God who lets people hurt?* must be changed. The real question is, *Can we pray to a God who died for people who hurt?*

In Christ God suffered alone, utterly and completely alone, so that you and I would *never* have to suffer alone. "Never will I leave you; never will I forsake you" (Heb 13:5). Because he was made like us in all respects when he suffered, he is able to sympathize with our weakness and will provide mercy and grace to help in times of need (Heb 2:14-18; 4:14-16). His concern for us is not measured by how much *our* pain might be reduced "if he really cared." Rather his sympathy is better evaluated in light of how much agony *he* endured on our behalf.

When the creation groans in the frustration of evil (Rom 8:19-22), when we groan in physical and emotional pain (2 Cor 5:2, 4) and are numbed speechless by our inability to understand (Rom 8:26), God hears (Ex 2:24; Judg 2:18; Ps 5:1). Through the Spirit who lives in us, he himself groans (Rom 8:26). God has not stayed a comfortable distance away, clucking and saying, "I told you so; you should have listened." As the body of Christ, Christians know that "if one part suffers, every part suffers with it" (1 Cor 12:26). Since we are united with Christ and since Christ is God, then when we suffer, *God himself suffers.*[15]

Through Christ, the Spirit, and brothers and sisters in the faith, God provides endurance and encouragement when we suffer. In the future, there is absolutely no doubt he will provide *complete victory* over evil, sin and death. In Jesus God has given us a basis for realistic hope . . . even when it hurts. This is what makes it possible for Paul to say, "We rejoice in the hope of the glory of God. Not only so, but we also rejoice in our sufferings" (Rom 5:2). *Hope* means that the cross is not just a statement about help and encouragement in the present. It is also, as Paul says in 1 Corinthians 15:57, an airtight guarantee of future victory over evil, sin and pain. Because of the cross, the day is coming when all evil will be answered with justice; all sin not forgiven through Christ will be punished. The day is coming when

the dwelling of God is with men, and he will live with them. They will be his people, and God himself will be with them and be their God. He will wipe every tear from their eyes. There will be no more death or mourning or crying or pain, for the old order of things has passed away. He who was seated on the throne said, "I am making everything new!" Then he said, "Write this down, for these words are trustworthy and true." (Rev 21:3-5)

This final certainty is what makes me desire to pray to a God who allows so many to hurt. When it hurts too much, I need you to pray for me.

Questions for Thought and Discussion

1. Do you think the existence of pain and evil is a difficulty for most praying Christians? Explain. Do you know anyone who has stopped praying because of suffering?

2. Wouldn't it be better to avoid thinking about ugly aspects of the world? Isn't that just what Paul says to do in Philippians 4:8?

3. What can be done for people who have become bitter toward God because of pain or evil?

4. "The results of love seem worth the risk of pain." Do you agree or disagree with this statement? Why or why not?

5. Do you think Christians feel they have to put on a happy face and have a nice day (every day) in order to be spiritual? Do you think your church or Bible study group lets people "hurt" in prayer?

6. What was your response to Joseph Bayly's prayer on p. 90?

7. Do you think God hurts when we hurt? What has God done about evil in the world and what are we supposed to do?

7
Father: Prayer as a Way of Life

Hillery, our five-year-old, was on the phone. She hesitantly explained that the bloodied feathers of a bird caught by the neighbor's cat were scattered on the lawn next to her playhouse. Sitting in my seminary office, I gazed out the window and pontificated: "Sometimes, honey, one animal has to die so another can live."

Hillery brightened a bit at my profundity and then chimed, "Oh, it's really all right though. It was *just* a Daddy bird . . ."

When I am tempted to feel useless and underrated as a father, I force myself to contemplate the fatherhood of God. The Bible uses images of both fathers and mothers to describe God, but fatherhood is the dominant image. Maybe fathers in ancient times also needed some encouragement for their tasks.

God as Father

In both testaments the Bible affirms that God as Creator is the natural Father of all men and women. From the prophets of Israel we hear: "O LORD, you are our Father. We are the clay, you are the potter; we are all the work of your hand" (Is 64:8); "Have we not all one Father? Did not one God create us?" (Mal 2:10). Paul's words in Acts 17 are better known: "The God who made the world and everything in it is the Lord of heaven and earth. . . . He himself gives all men life and breath and everything else. For in him we live and move and have our being. . . . 'We are his offspring' " (vv. 24-28). Every member of our race derives existence from God. He is the Father of us all. But he is also our Father in a different sense.

When Christians think of God as Father, we commonly think of our spiritual birth through faith in Christ: "Yet to all who received him, to those who believed in his name, he gave the right to become children of God—children born not of natural descent, nor of human decision or a husband's will, but born of God" (Jn 1:12-13).

According to Paul one of the evidences of being a spiritual child of God by faith is being able to call God Father when we pray: "Because you are sons, God sent the Spirit of his Son into our hearts, the Spirit who calls out, 'Abba, Father' " (Gal 4:5-6); "For you did not receive a spirit that makes you a slave again to fear, but you received the Spirit of sonship. And by him we cry, 'Abba, Father.' The Spirit himself testifies with our spirit that we are God's children" (Rom 8:15-16). But what does abba mean?

The Most Significant Word in Prayer

Abba is ancient Palestinian Aramaic baby talk meaning, "Dear Daddy." The rabbinic teachers of Israel used to say that when a child was weaned it began to say "Abba" and "Imma," words which exactly correspond to "Daddy" and "Mommy."[1] Thus abba derives from an intimate family relationship. It is a young child's word, though there is evidence that it continued to be used by adult sons and daughters, as "Daddy" and "Papa" are used today. The only other use of this Aramaic word in the Greek New Testament is in Mark 14:36 where Jesus prayed to God in Gethsemane as "Abba, Father." The presence of an Aramaic word in the New Testament Greek text is in itself rather unique. Though Jesus taught frequently in Aramaic, the evangelists have translated almost all of it into Greek. Even in early Christian Greek writing, abba is never used except in quotations of the three passages just mentioned.[2]

Exhaustive research by biblical scholars—particularly J. Jeremias and W. Marchel—has demonstrated that in all the huge literature of ancient Judaism there is not one instance of God being addressed in prayer with the word abba.[3] He was called "The Lord Almighty," "The Holy One," "Sovereign of the World" and many other exalted titles, but a word like abba was too personal, too familiar and intimate to be appropriate. The Lord was high and lifted up, the incomparable One. He was to be approached with reverence and awe. To call him "Daddy" was unthinkable blasphemy. Yet Jesus prayed like this all the time.

Scholars are convinced that if you listened to the prayers of the Lord Jesus, the characteristic initial expression would always be, "Abba."[4] Various forms of "Father" and "My Father" are taken as alternate Greek translations by the evangelists of Jesus' initial Aramaic abba. If Jesus prayed like this—which seems beyond reasonable doubt—we should understand abba as an expression of the completely unique sonship which he possessed as God's only begotten son. On Jesus' lips abba as an address to God in prayer is understandable and perhaps even expected. The amazing and unexpected thing is that he gave this privilege to ordinary men and women.

That Jesus gave Christians the right to address God as abba is usually argued from the wording of the Lord's Prayer (Lk 11:1-2). Asked to give his followers a way of praying which would be unique to his disciples, Jesus tells them to begin simply, "Father." The Greek word here is pater, the direct equivalent of the Aramaic abba. Jesus gave his disciples a privilege which previously had been his alone!

Yet to call God "Dear Father" does not seem special to most Christians. Many reading this have grown up, as I did, in communities where we heard God called "Father" from the earliest days of spiritual awareness. We need to be reminded periodically that the privilege of speaking with God so intimately was not given to even the greatest Old Testament saints.

The Pharasaic rabbis of Judaism stretched the Law to astounding limits, but none of them would have dared to call on God in prayer as *abba*. Being too familiar with God was serious business. They tried to kill Jesus for "calling God his own Father" (Jn 5:18). Yet one of the wonders of the salvation wrought by Jesus' death is the "adoption" into God's family of those who believe (Eph 1:5). Christians have been made "heirs of God and co-heirs with Christ" (Rom 8:17), and are now able to approach God without fear as beloved children.

The Abba Relationship

Abba represents the essentials of the new relationship with God which Jesus offered men and women who believe on his name. From the Father's side *abba* implies many things: (1) his mercy, compassion and love for the child; (2) his personal interest in the child and consistent concern for its good; (3) his willingness to provide for the needs of and give protection to the child; and (4) the use of his mature knowledge, judgment and wisdom in guiding and caring for the child. On the child's lips *abba* signifies (1) an implicit willingness to love, honor, and respect the Father; (2) an awareness of dependency on the Father; (3) a sense of confidence in the Father's judgment and trust in his integrity and abilities; and (4) ready obedience to the Father's desires and will, with corresponding acceptance of the Father's right and responsibility to discipline for the child's good. In short, *abba* signifies the essence of what it means to have a personal relationship with God.

Some of the best windows into understanding our Father-child relationship with God are found in biblical material which deals with human parenting. But the use of these texts tends to conjure up images from our home experiences. Because of this, we need to keep in mind that God is a *perfect* parent. And in him are combined all those positive attributes which on earth he has distributed between human mothers and fathers. As a perfect parent he acts— or does not act—*only* for our good. He does not treat his children in a particular way to meet his own needs or to compensate for some imbalance in his personality. He *never* acts to discourage or exasperate us. And he disciplines us in love, only for our good, and never to work out his own frustration or anger. But knowing these things are true doesn't always mean feeling they are.

No human father is perfect. And many of us have made serious mistakes at the emotional expense of our children. It will take some believers a period of time before negative feelings stop being associated with the word *father.* If this is true for you, ask God to help you forgive your human father or mother. I suspect you will find it hard to accept God as your perfect heavenly Father unless you do. I bring this up here because the rest of the chapter focuses on obedience. John said our heavenly Father's commands are not burdensome because his children obey as an act of love (1 Jn 5:3). But Christian obedience is a burden if your childhood has conditioned you to think that a parent must be obeyed to gain acceptance or avoid punishment. How can you respond in love to someone you're afraid will reject you or hurt you? It is not like this with our heavenly Father. "God has poured out his love into our hearts by the Holy Spirit, whom he has given us" (Rom 5:5), and that same Spirit frees us from this sort of slavery to fear and helps us to know God as "Abba, Father" (Rom 5:5; 8:15).

Reasons for Christian Obedience

As sovereign Lord, God has the right to expect our obedience to his commands. The remainder of this chapter centers on three teachings on obedience given special emphasis in the New Testament.

Obedience demonstrates to God that we love him. Humanity has an innate religiosity. In most of us this results in the feeling that love and devotion for God are best expressed by religious rituals of praise and worship. We believe that sacred acts somehow "get through" to God in a more significant way than does obedience in everyday living. But God apparently sees things the other way around. He asks:

> Does the LORD delight in burnt offerings and sacrifices
> as much as in obeying the voice of the LORD?
> To obey is *better* than sacrifice,
> and to heed is better than the fat of rams. (1 Sam 15:22, my emphasis)

Jesus expressed this idea in John 14: "If you love me, you will obey what I command. . . . If anyone loves me he will obey my teaching. . . . He who does not love me will not obey my teaching. These words you hear are not my own; they belong to the Father who sent me" (vv. 15, 23-24). Here Jesus claims that his teaching is the Father's. And any reader of the Gospels will soon discover that his teaching deals with attitudes and actions in *all* areas of life. The point is that to pray earnestly—"O Father, I love you. Thank you for loving me"—without active obedience to his word is unlikely to please him. "This is love for God: to obey his commands" (1 Jn 5:3).

In addition, *obedience proves to the world that we are God's children.* My neighbors learn things about my family by watching my children. And the same thing is true about the family of God. What we do as God's sons and daughters is the primary data on which those outside the family form opinions about our Father and his children. Thus Christian obedience is a means of identification. Knowing this, Paul said,

> Do all things without grumbling or disputing; that you may prove yourselves to be blameless and innocent, children of God above reproach in the midst of a crooked and perverse generation, among whom you appear as lights in the world. (Phil 2:14-15 NASB)

Paul followed the principle inherent in Jesus' teaching: "All men will know that you are my disciples if you love one another" (Jn 13:35). Most of us tend to think of obedience as a family affair, a matter between the Father and his children. But passages like these show that God's honor and the integrity of our family are also at stake. Obedience is directly tied to the credibility of the gospel. Obedience is essential to effective evangelism and the glorification of God: "Let your light shine before men, that they may see your good deeds and praise your Father in heaven" (Mt 5:16). Our obedience should cause *others* to offer praise and thanksgiving.

Finally, *obedience is a means God established to help us pray more effectively.* Jesus taught that Christian obedience and prayer are interrelated: "If you abide in Me, and My words abide in you, ask whatever you wish, and it shall be done for you" (Jn 15:7 NASB). Abiding in Christ is often explained in esoteric terms. But abiding is not mystical; rather it is moral and ethical.[5] John explains this clearly in his first letter: "We have confidence before God and receive from him anything we ask, *because* we obey his commands and do what pleases him. . . . Those who obey his commands live in him, and he in them" (1 Jn 3:21-24).

God will not encourage a disobedient lifestyle by giving answers to prayer. But the relationship between obedience and answered prayer is more complicated than that. We might think one "trades" or "pays for" answers to prayer in a currency called obedience. This sort of *quid pro quo* (this-for-that) arrangement is attractive because it reduces prayer and obedience to a mechanical system which can be used to our advantage. God becomes a kind of divine vending machine into which we must place units of obedience before pulling the lever through prayer which causes the answers to drop into our hands. Yet such a model is fundamentally flawed.

God's creatures, even those he has particularly loved, redeemed and given the privilege of calling him Abba, can never obligate or force his actions. This is acknowledged in Job, the oldest book in the Bible, and Paul applied the text in Job to the present age: "Who has ever given to God, that God should repay him?" (Rom 11:35). The clay simply cannot force the hand of the Potter.

Far from being a means to force God's hand, *obedience is a means God uses to train us to pray according to his will.* I have never seen this explained in a book on Christian prayer. But the link between obedience and prayer is clearly developed by Jesus in John 14—16. The basic text is this one:

> Whoever has my commands and obeys them, he is the one who loves me. He who loves me will be loved by my Father, and I too will love him and show myself to him. . . . If anyone loves me, he will obey my teaching. My Father will love him, and we will come to him and make our home with him. (Jn 14:21-23)

Obedience to Jesus' word facilitates fellowship with him and the Father. In the obedient believer Jesus and the Father make their "home" through the Holy Spirit: "This is how we know that he lives in us: We know it by the Spirit he gave us" (1 Jn 3:24). In the obedient believer the Spirit works to "show" (or "disclose") Jesus. Christ referred to this activity using several other concepts. He said the Spirit would "*teach* you all things and will *remind* you of everything I have said to you" (Jn 14:26); he will "*testify* about me" (15:26) and "*guide* you into all truth" (16:13). That this refers to growth in our understanding of the Father as well as Jesus is made clear in 16:14-15: "He will bring glory to me by taking from what is mine and making it known to you. All that belongs to the Father is mine. That is why I said the Spirit will take from what is mine and make it known to you."

Our obedience pleases God and creates in us an environment of love in which the Spirit encourages growth in our fellowship with, and understanding of, the Lord Jesus and his Father. As we come to know them better, we begin to see the world through God's eyes. As we learn to see existence God's way, we are enabled to pray according to his will. We are conditioned by obedience to internalize those principles of behavior which please God and are best for us.[6] This develops into the ability to make appropriate decisions in new situations or gray areas.

Parents inculcate moral values into their children. According to Proverbs 22:6, parents should train their children in the way they should go—that is, condition them to think the right way—so that when they are mature, they can make good decisions which do not deviate from what is right.

The Prayer-Obedience Cycle

Living according to God's will trains you to think in terms of God's will, and this helps you pray in God's will. The prayer-obedience relationship can be described as a cycle which perpetuates itself.[7]

Pray God's   Obey God's
Will   Will

Two things must be emphasized about this process. First, this "cycle" interacts with many other aspects of our Christian experience. There are many spiritual processes going on inside each of us, and we are also constantly interacting with our brothers and sisters in Christ. Second, this cycle does not constitute a method for getting answers to prayer. It is not a "system." Think about the process in a personal, not a mechanical, context. Our obedience does not guarantee answers to prayer. But the cycle does help a great deal in understanding how prayer effectiveness grows.

The authors of Scripture sometimes seem to assume such a process when they write about prayer. Psalm 37:4 is such a case: "Delight yourself in the LORD; and he will give you the desires of your heart." The author assumes one who delights in the Lord will also hide his word in their heart, meditate on it and seek to follow his statutes (Ps 119:11, 14-15). Delighting in the Lord thus changes the desires of our hearts into God's desires. The prayer-obedience process explains why God answers prayer offered by those who delight in him. Jesus is the most obvious example. His life shows how obedience and prayer fit together.

Jesus said, "Father, I thank you that you have heard me. I knew that you *always* hear me" (Jn 11:41-42). He also declared that "my food is to do the will of him who sent me" (Jn 4:34). Jesus' own words connect love, obedience and prayer: "I love the Father and . . . do exactly what my Father has commanded me. . . . If you remain in me and my words remain in you, ask whatever you wish, and it will be given you. . . . If you obey my commands you will remain in my love, just as I have obeyed my Father's commands and remain in his love" (Jn 14:31; 15:7, 10). And the relation of prayer and obedience is further confirmed by Hebrews 5:7-8, "During the days of Jesus' life on earth, he offered up prayers and petitions . . . and he was heard because of his reverent submission. Although he was a son, he learned obedience from what he suffered."

This relationship has several very practical implications. First, effectiveness in prayer will always be coupled with regular reading, memorizing of and meditating on Scripture. I see almost no potential to become a so-called prayer warrior where systematic Bible reading and study are absent. The Bible is the *only* divinely inspired guidebook to the will and thought of God. And learning to pray effectively boils down largely to learning to think like God and understanding his will. Read the Book.

Second, by now it should be apparent that the reason why the prayer of a righteous person is powerful and effective (Jas 5:16) is tied to the righteous person's commitment to *obey* God's Word. To pray effectively, you must obey.

Finally, the emphasis given to obedience in the passages we have considered makes it impossible to view prayer as a labor-saving device. God's children have no right to expect him to do in response to prayer what he has equipped them to do themselves. Prayer *and* obedience go together. And because effective prayer stems from obedience, prayer can never be viewed as a substitute for obedience. In the Bible God generally acts in response to prayer when he knows a situation is *beyond* the capabilities of his obedient children.

This chapter boils down to one simple but pointed question from Jesus: "Why do you call me, 'Lord, Lord,' and do not do what I say?" (Lk 6:46).

Questions for Thought and Discussion

1. Do you feel comfortable thinking about God as *Abba*, your "Dear Daddy"? Why or why not?
2. What does the concept of the fatherhood of God mean in your daily life?
3. How do our attitudes toward our parents affect the way we think about God?
4. What do you think about the contention that obedience to God's Word helps a Christian pray according to God's will?

5. Does the prayer-obedience cycle make sense to you? How does your experience confirm or undermine it?

6. If you could, what would you say to Jesus' question in Luke 6:46?

Part 2
How Should We Pray to Him?

8
Thanking:
The Prayer of
a Grateful Soul

A while back I had one of those days when everything
goes wrong. It began in the morning when I found a gray hair in
my moustache. As I leaned closer to the mirror to examine this
harbinger of senility, the other side of my 'stache got caught in the
triple rotary heads of my electric razor. And then I looked and saw
[that my] vanity [was scattered all over the top] of [the] vanity.

Later an earnest seminarian looked into my eyes and said (so
sincerely and *loudly*), "Prof, is there a book we could read that explains clearly just what you've been trying to say this past half-hour
or so?" I consoled myself with the sure knowledge that, come what
may, I was still an expert in a few matters theological, until I learned
that "an expert is one who knows more and more about less and

less until he knows absolutely everything about nothing." This new encouragement came to me courtesy of a page on the Murphy's Law Desk Calendar belonging to my best friend. As I contemplated the insignificance of my knowledge, I was tempted to feel that I really didn't know who I was or what I was supposed to be doing with my life.

Every person alive occasionally wonders, Just who am I? What am I here for anyway? The answer to the first question is that you are God's personal creation. You have been made in his image and have a unique combination of talents, skills and sensitivities not possessed by anyone else (see Ps 139:13-16; Gen 1:26-27; Jas 3:9). What is more, your continued existence at any given point in time is completely dependent on God's sustaining power through Christ (see Col 1:16-17; Heb 1:1-3). And this means that you are alive only because God wants you to be. Thus you matter and are valuable to him. In God's eyes, *you're somebody special.*[1]

Paul summarized these concepts saying, God "made the world and everything in it. . . . He himself gives all men life and breath and everything else. . . . 'For in him we live and move and have our being' " (Acts 17:24-25, 28). And since these ideas are based on the Word of God, they remain true, irrespective of whether you find it easy to feel this way about yourself or whether anybody else does either. Further, you can dismiss in good conscience "scientific" assertions that you are merely the chance result of a process which began between friendly protein molecules in some ancient, warm, soupy sea. And you can forgive the well-intentioned suggestions of hymn writers that you are nothing but a worthless worm. Knowing what you are is extremely important. Thinking you are the result of "random chance" or even a divinely designed night crawler often leads to acting like it.

But God made you and me, gave us personality, gifts, and his image, with something else in mind. Perhaps the best place in Scripture to find an indication of the purpose for human existence is Isaiah 43:6-7, where God says to Israel:

Bring my sons from afar

and my daughters from the ends of the earth—
everyone who is called by my name,
whom I created for my glory,
whom I formed and made.

This text is the basis for the famous interchange in the Westminster Shorter Catechism: "What is the chief end of man? Man's chief end is to glorify God, and to enjoy him forever."

What does it mean to glorify God? The Bible uses the term *glorify* to convey such ideas as,

- ☐ To honor
- ☐ To increase the fame of
- ☐ To make one's name great
- ☐ To extol the virtues of
- ☐ To magnify the reputation of
- ☐ To cause others to think positively about.

But the basic concept is well summed up in the doxology which begins, "Praise God from whom all blessings flow, Praise him all creatures here below." In a practical sense glorifying God boils down to *blessing* his name, that is *praising* his greatness and perfection. It means living a life characterized by *thanksgiving.*

Why Glorify God?

In an ultimate theological sense, God is to be glorified simply because of the splendor and perfection of his own nature and character. He is personally worth it and deserves our glorification: "Great is the LORD and most worthy of praise; his greatness no one can fathom" (Ps 145:3). But there are other reasons.

First, we glorify God because we exist. God did not have to create anything, particularly you or me. God should be glorified by his creatures because he made them. It is far better to be—no matter how painful one's existence—than not to be at all.

You are worthy, our Lord and God,
to receive glory and honor and power,
for you created all things,
and by your will they were created

and have their being. (Rev 4:11)

Second, in creating humanity God did a great work. He could have made us without his image, without personality or abilities such as thinking or communication. Yet he gave every one of us a great deal more.

You made him a little lower than the heavenly beings
and crowned him with glory and honor.
You made him ruler over the works of your hands;
you put everything under his feet. (Ps 8:5-6)

Because we have been given much more than mere existence, the psalmist concludes, "O LORD, our Lord, how majestic is your name in all the earth!" (v. 9).

Paul argues in Romans 1 that given such facts, God's power and divinity are plain and clearly seen by all men and women, "being understood from what has been made" (v. 20). He refers to that evidence about God's character seen in nature (Job 36:22—39:30; Ps 8:3); the sun and rain (Mt 5:45); the seasons (Acts 14:15-17); human nature (Ps 139:14) and history (Acts 17:26-27). This evidence, Paul assumes, is sufficient for each man and woman to understand the fact of God's existence and our creaturely obligation to glorify him. But he goes on to say that we can—and do—suppress this truth and live in sin as if there were no God and we were all spontaneously generated and self-existent: "Although they knew God, they neither glorified him as God nor gave thanks to him. . . . They exchanged the truth of God for a lie, and worshiped and served created things rather than the Creator—who is forever praised. Amen" (Rom 1:21, 25). To the question, Why should I glorify God? Paul answers, "In him you live, move and exist!" God's creatures are obliged to acknowledge and glorify him. Neither pain and hurt, nor success and greatness produce any exceptions. An ancient saying from Pharisaic Judaism summarizes all of this: "He that gets enjoyment out of the world without giving thanks, has committed a sacrilege; he has defrauded the Lord."[2]

Finally, Christians glorify God because to the blessing of existence he has added the countless blessings of salvation and a covenant relationship with him. He has not only made us; he has loved us! In Christ we have been redeemed from the terrible penalty of our sin and made co-heirs with Christ of eternal riches (Rom 3:23-24; Gal 4:4-7; Eph 1:3-8). By the blood of Jesus and the power of the Holy Spirit, the Almighty Creator has become our dear Father (Jn 1:12-13; 3:5; Rom 8:15-17). In Christ we know him now as one "who is able to keep you from falling and to present you before his glorious presence without fault and with great joy" (Jude 24). As Christians, we "are A CHOSEN RACE, A royal PRIESTHOOD, A HOLY NATION, A PEOPLE FOR *God's* OWN POSSESSION, *that you may proclaim the excellencies of Him* who has called you out of darkness into His marvelous light" (1 Pet 2:9 NASB).

But I Don't Feel Like Glorifying God

Most Christians do not break out in spontaneous praise to God, nor do we function most days with an attitude of thanksgiving. Often we simply forget who God is, what he has done, the constancy of his love for us and the certainty of our salvation. But the problem is heightened by the nature of modern existence.

First, because we live in an age characterized by the power of negative thinking and a constant (and carefully calculated) sense of personal dissatisfaction, we do not feel grateful.

What we are, possess and have experienced are never quite enough. There are always others with whom we can compare ourselves. Media advertisers and image makers daily exploit the insecurity resulting from our lack of personal beauty, charm, intellect, strength, talented children, clothing, expensive cars, popular toys, exciting vacations, large homes, academic degrees, satisfying careers and meaningful relationships. It is hard to feel glad that God made you, if you wish he had made you white instead of black, tall instead of short, or smarter than just plain average. Who can rejoice in having the strength to work when your job is terrible and pays so poorly? What is so special about being able to see if your TV's only black and white? And why be thankful for your husband's faithfulness if he is so fat nobody else would want him? What good is being able to laugh if you are usually the one being laughed at?

Everyone knows something of this sense of personal inadequacy and dissatisfaction. Low self-esteem can cause two apparently opposite mental and spiritual conditions. One is depression and personal isolation; the other is vanity and public ostentation. Our dissatisfaction grows into the suspicion that God has not been doing as much for us as he should have. Since we are certain that we are at least as deserving as someone else, we become bitter at not receiving the same blessing. Eventually we reach the conclusion, "You can't really depend on God." At this point negative feelings may overwhelm us, or we may get angry: "You've got to look out for yourself and be self-sufficient. I'll show you, you wait and see." Either way we end up in a corner. The first corner is unrealistic self-deprecation: "Nobody loves me." The second corner is unhealthy self-aggrandizement: "Hey, look at me."

Thankfulness is rare in either situation. Thankfulness introduces God into our thinking, and that requires re-evaluating our attitude toward ourselves. Thankfulness grows in an *honest* heart which, after confessing the sin of self-pity, accepts the present situation and presses on toward God's goal (see 1 Cor 15:10; Phil 3:13-14). Thankfulness finds room in a *humble* heart which, after confessing the sin of self-sufficiency, seeks to acknowledge God's activity in all of life (see Prov 3:6; Jn 3:27).

The spirit of our age—especially much modern advertising—actively wars within our minds against the spirit of thankfulness. It turns appreciation for the diversity of our gifts and skills into a comparison mentality (the "pecking order"). It focuses attention on people as if they were objects for display rather than unique creations. It devalues those qualities of inner beauty in favor of outward glamor. If we are taken in, we end up worshiping and serving created things, not God. Does it help or hinder the desire to say grace over a hamburger to know that "you *deserve* a break today" and "You're the one. We do it all for *you*"?

If you want to glorify God, you *have to* be aware of this kind of mind manipulation. You must constantly think against the grain of

modern existence: it is God "who has made us, and not we ourselves" (Ps 100:3 NASB).

Second, we find it hard to be thankful because of the pace of
modern life. Many people are so busy that there isn't much time
to think, let alone count our blessings. Part of the remedy here is
a re-examination of how we spend our time. Some may be helped
by learning to be more efficient. But others must give up the idea
that Christian busyness is next to godliness. Jesus was speaking of
a small oil lamp when he said, "Let your light shine before men,
that they may see your good deeds and praise your Father in heav-
en" (Mt 5:16). Such lamps gave off a small amount of light over
several hours and then the wick had to be trimmed and more oil
added. But the velocity of many modern Christian experiences
makes our "light" more like the pulsating of a strobe. Do you want
your life to provide enough steady light so that others can see God,
or are you merely hustling to draw attention to yourself? Ask God
to help you think through the motivation behind your busyness.

Third, gratitude sometimes eludes us because the ugliness of life
around us makes it difficult to remember God's gifts. Hiking in the
mountains encourages my sense of creatureliness. Psalm 8 seems
relevant when I'm walking by the sea. But many Christians have
never been on a beach nor seen a mountain wilderness. Some
children have never caught a fish or touched a buttercup. (Fish, as
all urbanites know, are small rectangular things, about ½" x 1" x
4", covered with bread crumbs. Bread, made of flour which needs
vitamin enriching, comes from panel trucks and grows in plastic
bags.) In the world God called very good, the sky was not brown
from NO_x emissions, and the raindrops that fell didn't kill fish. It
is hard to find God in the concrete, steel and plastic in which modern man lives, moves and has his being.

Yet despite the effects of human sin, the creation still points to
its Creator. And it is important for anyone who wants to keep man
and God in right perspective to get out of the city occasionally and
to help others—especially children—to see something green that is
not covered with trash or paint. Maybe in your circumstances a

book, travelog or just a potted plant on the window ledge will have
to suffice. But keep reminding yourself that men and cities pass
away, the Sphinx has lost its nose and the Parthenon is being eaten
up by smog. Though it seems we live in urban areas without any
need for, or reminders of, God's existence, the truth is otherwise.

Lord, you have been our dwelling place
    throughout all generations.
Before the mountains were born
    or you brought forth the earth and the world,
    from everlasting to everlasting you are God. (Ps 90:1-2)

Finally, there will be times when personal pain and the suffering of
others causes us to suppress the truth of God's goodness and our
thankfulness. When that happens, a glib, "Well, praise the Lord
anyhow," is not the answer. Ask God to protect your heart from
bitterness, take away your anger, and replace it with a spirit of
submission. Call on God in truth. Don't whistle in the dark. Peter's
advice concerning such hurt is, "Humble yourselves, therefore, under God's mighty hand, that he may lift you up in due time. Cast
all your anxiety on him because he cares for you. . . . Your brothers
throughout the world are undergoing the same kind of sufferings"
(1 Pet 5:6-7, 9). Through Christ there is grace to help us in time of
need. For this we *can* be thankful.

What You Pray and What You Are

We all have a tendency to think of thanksgiving as something you
say when you pray. Yet Jesus said, "Father . . . I have brought you
glory on earth by completing the work you gave me to do" (Jn 17:4).
The same idea is found in Paul's "whatever you do, do it all for the
glory of God" (1 Cor 10:31). This concept—which has deep roots in
Judaism—is that one's *life is a prayer*. (This thought may help explain
how Christians might pray *at all times* as we are instructed in Ephesians 6:18.)

    As you think about glorifying God, begin to think about your
entire life as a thank offering presented in gratitude to God. "This
is to my Father's glory, that you bear much fruit, showing your-

selves to be my disciples" (Jn 15:8). With the help of God's Spirit, resolve to *be a prayer of thanksgiving*. Glorify him every day through your "love, joy, peace, patience, kindness, goodness, faithfulness, gentleness and self-control" (Gal 5:22-23). Beause of who you are, no one can do it better. And that *is* what God made you for.

Questions for Thought and Discussion

1. Do you believe that to God "you're somebody special"? Why or why not?
2. What are you most thankful for right now? Do you think that what we feel thankful for changes as we go through life?
3. What hinders wanting to count your blessings?
4. Why is materialism a threat to glorifying God?
5. How does media advertising encourage dissatisfaction and insecurity?
6. What do you think about the author's claim that "life is a prayer"?
7. What can you do to encourage somebody else to thank and glorify God? Who can you do this with next week? How are you going to go about it?

9
Responding:
The Prayer of a
Chastened Disciple

Doug's red hair was sodden with sweat and plastered to his forehead, which had turned completely white. His bicycle, made of high-strength, light-metal alloys, was in fairly good shape. Doug, made of things like raisins, crunchy peanut butter and piña colada yogurt, was not so well off.

As I watched the doctor removing bits of the road from my son's arm and legs I kept wondering, "I'm sure I prayed for his safety. Why do things like this have to happen?" Actually, there were some rather good answers.

Doug had been negotiating a mud patch on a turn, going downhill on a mountain road at 30 miles per hour. On a cycle with tires which have only two to four square inches of surface in contact with the road, you simply can't do that. The laws of physics, specifically friction, inertia and centrifugal force, were responsible for the accident. Doug was wiped out by Sir Isaac Newton!

But, of course, that was not the whole story: the experience was full of learning. Doug knew about the value of protective equipment from books and ads and had talked with friends who had cycling accidents. But the importance of a fiberglass helmet and leather gloves had now sunk in quite deeply. No amount of talking and reading made the impact the crash did. And there were other intangible results.

Through the pain Doug moved significantly closer to maturity and responsibility. The accident put other scrapes and traumas in a different perspective. Within days the "agony" attached to his cross-country team workouts diminished noticeably. A few weeks later he picked up and carried his younger sister about eight blocks after she fell and skinned both knees. He also gained confidence. He now knows experientially certain things about capabilities and limits: his own and those of his machine. And there was something learned about the contingency of existence. Life does not always go as planned, and even diligent training and good equipment won't stop mud patches from appearing where you don't expect them.

Truth or Consequences

Doug's accident was one of those experiences which result from the way God made the world. His fall was simply a consequence of reality, and such happenings are morally neutral. It is neither right nor wrong that thin bike tires + mud + sufficient velocity = inadequate friction to keep a bike on the road. Christians have a tendency to turn such *consequences* into *judgments*. (If something bad happens, God must be punishing me.)[1]

I don't think Doug's injuries were a punishment for going too fast down the mountain. This was Doug's first encounter with mud on a turn on a mountain road, and lack of experience is neither morally culpable nor a sin requiring retribution. But Doug's heavenly Father has used the incident—as he desires to use all our life experiences—

to discipline and teach Doug principles which transcend those of physics and cycling.

Because God created an orderly universe, there are principles which explain how both the material (physical) and immaterial (spiritual) realms function.[2] As inadequate friction will cause a wheel to skid, so breaking God's moral law will result in guilt and condemnation before God. Sin also results in other consequences. For example, the sin of vanity and pride may result personally in poor judgment, interpersonally in driving others away from you, and theologically in the hindrance of your prayers. Principles in the spiritual realm are just as "concrete" as those observed by scientists in the physical disciplines, though we tend to forget this because we cannot measure them with rulers and stopwatches.

Scripture teaches us the principles God has established in the spiritual realm. Human experience reinforces these principles. But as everybody knows, a lot of learning comes from making mistakes. And God teaches us many principles by disciplining us when we make mistakes.

Discipline and Prayer

How does all this relate to prayer? *First*, some of the greatest factors affecting our willingness, desire and attitude in prayer are our reactions to the events God allows or sends into our lives. Pain and prayer are connected in many different ways.

Second, if obedience helps us pray in harmony with God's will, disobedience hinders it. Because he cares and wants to respond to our prayers, God often directs us back to the way of obedience through discipline. His discipline functions a little like warning signs and guard rails on a highway. Discipline helps us avoid serious spiritual collisions and keeps us from running too far off the narrow way (of obedience) which leads to life and fellowship with God.

Prayer and discipline, then, are interrelated. But discipline is *greatly* misunderstood. We all have a tendency to think of discipline as punishment or retribution which comes as a consequence of doing wrong. But five minutes with a concordance will show that the biblical words translated "discipline," "chastise," "chasten" and "chastisement" are primarily Hebrew and Greek terms which refer to *learning*, not retribution. In well over ninety per cent of the cases the words literally mean "teach," "instruct," "train up," "point out," "make obvious" or "bring conviction about." The Bible never says such learning is convenient or fun, but it is necessary and universal in the family of God. And since discipline is a learning experience from which no believer ever "graduates" this side of heaven, Christians who feel that discipline is punishment can easily believe that God is angry and displeased with them most of the time. And no one wants to talk with someone who is always mad at them, and so we stop talking to God.

Becoming "Goal Oriented"

Repeatedly, as I watch the feats of strength and endurance displayed by Olympic athletes I am impressed with the years of difficult training it takes to perform so brilliantly. These men and women are living illustrations of what Paul spoke of in 1 Corinthians 9:24-27:

Do you not know that in a race all the runners run, but only one gets the prize? Run in such a way as to get the prize. Everyone who competes in the games goes into strict training. They do it to get a crown that will not last; but we do it to get a crown that will last forever. Therefore I do not run like a man running aimlessly; I do not fight like a man beating the air. No, I beat my body and make it my slave.

Athletes accept discipline because they know that the goal (the "prize") is worth training for. They understand that the coach who plans their workouts wants to help them reach their full potential and obtain the goal.

Christians are also in a race, a race whose goal is Christlikeness. And as we work out we need to focus on the *goal* (being like Jesus), not the race or the training. Further, we must remember that the Coach is on our side (Rom 8:31) and has planned it so that we will win (Rom 8:29; Phil 3:14). Strict training, as Paul implies, is likely to hurt. "No pain, no gain" is the motto of many athletes. The same is true in the Christian life, but submitting to discipline is easier for athletes than for Christians. In athletics the goals are tangible, the way to them is understood and their achievement is measurable. For believers none of these may be true.

Having made the "pursuit of happiness" a personal goal and in one case a national right, Christians in the West have come to expect happiness, peace and security in life. Those who might raise questions about this—the chronically and terminally ill, for example—are quietly tucked away behind clean white walls, out of sight and out of the way. But Paul said, "I consider that our present sufferings are not worth comparing with the glory that will be revealed in us" (Rom 8:18). Paul assumes that it is normal to suffer. Peter says that Christians are called by God to suffer (1 Pet 2:21). Yet an astounding number of Christians today seem to figure that the discipline through which God works—the physical and mental suffering, hardship, persecution, grief, adversity and so on—is simply not intended for us. When our pursuit of happiness is disrupted, we grow depressed and convinced that God has turned his back on us. If difficulty persists we know in the depths of our souls that prayer doesn't "work": we *begged* God to kiss away our hurt . . . and he didn't.

The measure of God's love, however, is *not* inversely proportional to the amount of pain, adversity and tribulation we may be called to endure. And the efficacy of prayer *cannot* be measured by how much suffering may be reduced by earnest petition.

Accepting discipline will foster spiritual growth, encourage prayer and glorify God. But these goals are hard to keep in mind today when life is viewed so differently. Bible translator J. B. Phillips described how the attitudes of the New Testament authors differed from ours today:

To the writers of [the New Testament epistles] this present life was only an incident. It was lived, with a due sense of responsibility, as a preface to sharing the timeless life of God himself. To these men this world was only a part, and because of the

cumulative result of human sin a highly infectious part, of God's
vast created universe, seen and unseen. They trained themselves
therefore, and attempted to train others, not to be "taken in" by
this world, not to give their hearts to it, not to conform to its
values, but to remember constantly that they were only tempo-
rary residents, and that their rights of citizenship were in the
unseen world of Reality. Today when all the emphasis is thrown
upon making the most of this life, and even Christianity is only
seriously considered in many quarters because of its social implications, this point of view is comparatively rarely held.[3]
Yet toward this very attitude God pushes us through discipline.
"Look not at the things which are seen, but at the things which are
not seen; for the things which are seen are temporal, but the things
which are not seen are eternal" (2 Cor 4:18 NASB). Growing up
changes the way you think about life, but it does not make you
immune to pain. What's hard to take is that discipline *hurts*.

Discipline: God's Megaphone or His Whip?
God works through discipline—especially suffering—to get our attention and reorient us. Such a realignment of values and attitudes
is a matter of life and death: eternal life or eternal death. For unbelievers the focus is on attaining salvation through faith in Christ.
For believers the concern is living consistently (obediently) with the
eternal life already possessed. Our Lord's use of discipline is directed
toward *becoming* a spiritual child of God and *living* like one.

C. S. Lewis has cogently explained the reasons for the fact that
discipline has to hurt. In *The Problem of Pain* he says:
The human spirit will not even begin to try to surrender self-will
as long as all seems to be well with it. Now error and sin both
have this property that the deeper they are the less their victim
suspects their presence. . . .
We can rest contentedly in our sins and in our stupidities. . . .
But pain insists on being attended to. God whispers to us in our
pleasures, speaks in our conscience, but shouts in our pains: it is
His megaphone to rouse a deaf world. A bad man, happy, is a

man without the least inkling that his actions . . . are not in accord with the laws of the universe.⁴

I do not like what Lewis says. But I am convinced he is right. The facts of human history show that we usually question our self-sufficiency only when *forced* to look up to heaven. We begin seriously to consider the state of our relationship with God only because we are emotionally or physically flat on our backs. I have pulled enough doors marked "Push" in three-inch letters to know that sometimes I do have to be hit in the face to get my attention.

Yet if God's discipline is just, we might reply, why do good people often experience great pain while many evil persons seem to "get away with murder." Consider this: if two people float downriver and one person's craft is holed by a submerged rock, is the wet, bruised and bedraggled soul who crawls ashore having lost all the gear in the boat better or worse off than the other person, who is dashed to pulp on the rocks below the hidden waterfall? If God stops you through some traumatic discipline from "getting away with" a course of action which may eventually destroy you or those you love, *thank him* for being concerned enough to stop you. That he may allow others to float effortlessly by your discomfort to an end that he alone knows is hardly adequate ground on which to question his justice.

We must get rid of the notion that discipline is punishment. When God chastises, he speaks in love, not justice. If he responded in justice whenever we sinned we would be constantly terrorized: "It is a dreadful thing to fall into the hands of the living God" (Heb 10:31). Nevertheless, most of us still feel like Job, who said, "I am innocent, but God denies me justice. . . . It profits a man nothing when he tries to please God' " (Job 34:5, 9). So to understand discipline we, like Job, must hear the Lord's reply:

But I tell you, in this [complaint] you are not right,
    for God is greater than man.
Why do you complain to him
    that he answers none of man's words?

For God does speak—now one way, now another—
    though man may not perceive it.
in a dream, in a vision of the night,
    when deep sleep falls on men
    as they slumber in their beds,
he may speak in their ears
    and terrify them with warnings,
to turn man from wrongdoing
    and keep him from pride,
to preserve his soul from the pit,
    his life from perishing by the sword.
Or a man may be chastened on a bed of pain
    with constant distress in his bones,
so that his very being finds food repulsive
    and his soul loathes the choicest meal.
His flesh wastes away to nothing,
    and his bones, once hidden, now stick out.
His soul draws near to the pit,
    and his life to the messengers of death.

Yet if there is an angel on his side
    as a mediator, one out of a thousand,
    to tell a man what is right for him,
to be gracious to him and say,
    "Spare him from going down to the pit;
    I have found a ransom for him"—
then his flesh is renewed like a child's;
    it is restored as in the days of his youth.
He prays to God and finds favor with him,
    he sees God's face and shouts for joy;
    he is restored by God to his righteous state.
Then he comes to men and says,
    "I sinned, and perverted what was right,
    but I did not get what I deserved.
He redeemed my soul from going down to the pit,

and I will live to enjoy the light."

God does all these things to a man—
twice, even three times—
to turn back his soul from the pit,
    that the light of life may shine on him. (Job 33:12-30)

When God redeems our souls from the pit it is not punishment.

Theologically, punishment is the just response of a holy God to the sin and guilt of his creatures. In a technical sense, punishment is the lot only of those who reject God's saving grace and die as unbelievers. It is retribution for what has been done in the past and is especially associated with our final judgment before God. In a word, punishment is hell.

Discipline, chastisement and rebuke, on the other hand, are the loving (and *not* wrathful) responses of a holy Creator. Perhaps most often they are his concerned reaction to our sin, but there are also times when discipline does not seem to be the result of moral wrong. In these cases God may have spiritual maturity and character development in mind when he allows suffering.[5] God's discipline, chastisement and rebuke are oriented toward the *future*, toward spiritual life and its development. God chastens and rebukes *all* men and women because he is not willing that any should perish and come to the terror of the "pit"; and he wants all to come to spiritual truth.

But the word *discipline* has its primary context in the family. It expresses a parent's concern to train and develop values and characteristics which are in the child's best interest. God always has these goals in mind with believers, his spiritual children. All of us tend to use the words loosely, but discipline, not punishment, seems the more apt term for the Father's love.

God's spiritual children by faith are *never* punished. As Isaiah 53 says, their "stripes" were taken completely by Christ. God is not mad at believers when he disciplines them after they sin. His personal offense, his righteous anger, his wrath, was vented wholly and completely on Jesus at Calvary. We never suffer to make up some portion of punishment for our sin. God disciplines us, but never in anger, never in rage, and always in love with compassion. Knowing this doesn't make God's discipline hurt less, but knowing he cares helps.[6]

We make it difficult for God as well as ourselves when we stop talking to him—stop praying—during times of discipline and pain. Contrary to what we think, God is *very* close when it hurts. He says, "Here I am! I stand at the door and knock. If anyone hears my voice and opens the door, I will go in and eat with him, and he with me" (Rev 3:20). He does not say, "Go away until you can be good." In Christ he has chosen to make us good himself.

God's discipline is an unmistakable sign that he loves and values us. C. S. Lewis writes,

> The Church is the Lord's bride whom He so loves that in her no spot or wrinkle is endurable (Eph. [5:]27). . . . The truth which this analogy serves to emphasise is that Love, in its own nature, demands the perfecting of the beloved. . . . When we fall in love with a woman, do we cease to care whether she is clean or dirty, fair or foul? . . . Does any woman regard it as a sign of love in a man that he neither knows or cares how she is looking? . . . To ask that God's love should be content with us as we are is to ask that God should cease to be God: because He is what He is, His love must, in the nature of things, be impeded and repelled, by certain stains in our present character, and because He already loves us He must labor to make us lovable.[7]

Someone who loves and values you this much will not go away if you decide to stop talking to him when it hurts, but you miss a great deal by staying in spiritual seclusion. Even if you feel your adversity is his rebuke for some sin, he still wants to talk with you. Try to hear his voice and open the door to communication and fellowship once again. And try to understand God's purposes in your struggle.

Why Discipline?
There are a number of reasons why God disciplines us. The first

is the one we've already looked at: God disciplines us to encourage *obedience*. And, as we've already seen in the prayer-obedience cycle, obedience is intimately connected with our prayer lives. As we obey, our prayer lives bear fruit. And as we pray we grow to know God better and can obey him more and so on . . .

Second, God disciplines us to help us develop *godly personality characteristics*. Paul writes, "We also rejoice in our sufferings, because we know that suffering produces perseverance; perseverance, character; and character, hope" (Rom 5:3-4). The writer to the Hebrews says that "God disciplines us for our good, that we may share in his holiness. . . . It produces a harvest of righteousness and peace for those who have been trained by it" (Heb 12:10-11). And James asks us to "consider it pure joy, my brothers, whenever you face trials of many kinds, because you know that the testing of your faith develops perseverance. Perseverance must finish its work so that you may be mature and complete, not lacking anything" (Jas 1:2-4). God's ultimate objective is our spiritual maturity, complete conformity to the image of Christ.

Further, God's discipline is intended to result in *increased fruitfulness*. In John 15:1 Jesus calls the Father "the gardener" and describes his discipline of obedient believers as "vine dressing": "every branch that bears fruit, He prunes it, *that it may bear more fruit*" (15:2 NASB). The older growth removed from a fruitful vine is not necessarily bad or infected. The fact is that fruit bearing is especially associated with new growth. So fruit plants (and Christians) are pruned.

Your business may fail, then, not because of sin or mismanagement on your part, but because God wants you to be doing something else. You can respond with prayer focused on the past: "Why, why did you take away what I've worked all my life to build up?" Or you can anticipate new growth and fruitfulness and say: "This hurts. You know how hard I've worked. But what do you want me to do now? Show me the way, and I'll try to walk in it."

Such pruning also refines our motives in obedience. Things can sometimes go so well—because we seek to live ethically, for example—that we begin to enjoy the easy life *more* than submitting to

God's Word. We obey for the wrong reasons: only because we like the consequences.

Fourth, *dependency on God* is often reinforced through discipline. When things go well we tend to forget God, and when we enjoy success we often feel we have achieved it ourselves. Paul speaks in 2 Corinthians 12:7 of suffering brought into his life "to keep me from becoming conceited."

In addition, through discipline God confirms *genuine faith*. Not that God wonders whether we are true believers. On the contrary, he wants to prove publicly through a test, trial or temptation what he *already* knows is there. God said to the devil with a father's obvious pride in his child: "Have you considered my servant Job? There is no one on earth like him; he is blameless and upright, a man who fears God and shuns evil" (Job 1:8).

The story goes on, as you know, and the devil gets permission to take away Job's family, his riches and his health. Yet Job met the temptation to curse God and die with reason: "Shall we accept good from God, and not trouble?" (2:10). As a result he has been remembered throughout history as the man who spoke what is right about God in spite of all the trouble the Lord had brought upon him (42:7-11). He passed the test . . . as God knew he would all along.

Sixth, through discipline we learn *spiritual truth*. The famous text in Hebrews 5:8 says that Jesus learned through what he suffered, and it is obvious at several points that Job's suffering was instructional. Early in Israel's history the Lord spoke through Moses saying,

> Remember how the LORD your God led you all the way in the desert these forty years. . . . He humbled you, causing you to hunger and then feeding you with manna . . . *to teach you* that man does not live by bread alone but on every word that comes from the mouth of the LORD. . . . Know then in your heart that as a man disciplines his son, so the LORD your God disciplines you. (Deut 8:2-3, 5)

Finally, in discipline *God reveals his glory and ours*. In John 11 Lazarus died, and his sisters went through profound grief, according to

Jesus, "for God's glory so that God's Son may be glorified through it" (v. 4). In John 9 we are told that a man (an unbeliever, interestingly) was born blind "so that the work of God might be displayed in his life" (v. 3). Peter implies a similar notion when he tells Christians being persecuted by pagans to "live such good lives among the pagans that, though they accuse you of doing wrong, they may see your good deeds and glorify God" (1 Pet 2:12).

This is perhaps the hardest discipline of all, because apart from divine revelation those undergoing this kind of suffering may not know what it is all about.

The glory of God, not our happiness, is what we exist for. Humanity is not the center of things, and God does not exist for our sake. We don't even exist for our own sake. We exist for God's sake, his glory. His promise is that after our Lord has glorified himself through us, we shall, in fact, know happiness and glory ourselves. In Peter's words,

> Dear friends, do not be surprised at the painful trial you are suffering, as though something strange were happening to you. But rejoice that you participate in the sufferings of Christ, so that *you may be overjoyed* when his glory is revealed. If you are insulted because of the name of Christ, you are blessed, for the Spirit of glory and of God rests on you. (1 Pet 4:12-14)

And who can forget Paul's anticipation?

> We are hard pressed on every side, but not crushed; perplexed, but not in despair; persecuted, but not abandoned; struck down, but not destroyed. . . . *Our light and momentary troubles are achieving for us an eternal weight of glory that far outweighs them all.* (2 Cor 4:8-9, 17)

Clearly there *are* good reasons, then, to "be joyful in hope, patient in affliction, faithful in prayer" (Rom 12:12).

Questions for Thought and Discussion

1. Think of a situation in which God seems to have disciplined you. What did you learn from it?

2. The author says that discipline is not the same thing as punishment or judgment.

Do you think Scripture supports this notion?

3. Why does it matter whether discipline comes from one who loves us?

4. The author says "no pain, no gain" is a principle which applies to our spiritual lives. What do you think about this? Do you have to hurt to be holy?

5. Is suffering part of the normal Christian life? What evidence from the Bible and life supports your response?

6. Have you ever felt that God was mad at you? When and why?

7. Why do Christians find it hard to accept the notion that God's discipline is really evidence that God loves them?

10
Loving:
The Prayer for
Other People

There's a prayer stuck on the wall, right at eye level, in front of my desk:

> LORD, make me an instrument of Thy peace:
>> where there is hatred, let me sow love;
>> where there is injury, pardon;
>> where there is doubt, faith;
>> where there is despair, hope;
>> where there is darkness, light;
>> and where there is sadness, joy.

These words are traditionally attributed to St. Francis of Assisi. I have found the prayer is personally very significant. For a long time, I've wondered: What is the "essence" of Christianity? its very heart?

My conclusion: LOVE. But "love" has become nearly meaningless in the twentieth century. Where I live the word stands for fuzzy pastel teddy bears, a barbecue restaurant, a wedding apparel shop . . . and pornography. How, I've wondered, can I visualize Christian love? This question was answered by St. Augustine of Hippo. "What does love look like?" he said. "It has the hands to help others. It has the feet to hasten to the poor and needy. It has eyes to see misery and want. It has the ears to hear the sighs and sorrows of men. That is what love looks like." The words on my office wall, I've discovered, are love turned into prayer.

In the Bible also love and prayer are directly linked with one another. This chapter explores the how and why of this vital relationship.

God Is Love

Even the newest Christian soon comes to know that "God is love" (1 Jn 4:8). Over and over the Bible tells us of God's love: "I have loved you with an everlasting love; I have drawn you with loving-kindness" (Jer 31:3); "God demonstrates his own love for us in this: While we were still sinners, Christ died for us" (Rom 5:8). In biblical thinking the essence of divinity is love.

The appropriate response to this love is for God's people to love in return. Talking about the Old Testament, Jesus said, "All the Law and the Prophets hang on these two commandments" (Mt 22:40): "Love the Lord your God with all your heart and with all your soul and with all your mind," and, "Love your neighbor as yourself" (vv. 37, 39). Paul asserted that "the entire law is summed up in a single command: 'Love your neighbor as yourself' " (Gal 5:14). "Therefore love is the fulfillment of the law" (Rom 13:10). There is no tension between Paul and Jesus here. Paul simply assumes something Jesus made explicit elsewhere: *You love God by loving other people.*

The night before he died, Jesus said, "A new commandment I give you: Love one another. As I have loved you, so you must love one another. All men will know that you are my disciples if you love one another" (Jn 13:34-35). This commandment is repeated twice more during the following discourse (Jn 15:12, 17). Jesus' disciples are to be characterized by his selfless love. "This is how we know what love is: Jesus Christ laid down his life for us. And we ought to lay down our lives for our brothers" (1 Jn 3:16). The commandment to love is both old (always a part of true religion for those who have worshiped the God of Israel) and new (never before so clearly illustrated and enabled prior to Christ). For Jesus, love was a four-letter word which summed up the essence of being a Christian.

Love and its result, Christian unity, are essential to the credibility of Christianity. People who bear the message of God's love must love one another. The apostle John was particularly clear on this point in his Gospel and letters: "Everyone who loves has been born of God and knows God. Whoever does not love does not know God" (1 Jn 4:7-8). "If anyone says, 'I love God,' yet hates his brother, he is a liar. For anyone who does not love his brother, whom he has seen, cannot love God, whom he has not seen. And he has given us this command: Whoever loves God must also love his brother" (1 Jn 4:20-21; see also 3:10, 14-15).

Love and Prayer

The gist of John's message is obvious. If you are not expressing love to Christian brothers and sisters, you have no right to claim to be God's child, to call him Abba, or to expect him to respond to your prayers. As the body without the spirit is dead and faith without deeds is dead, so *prayer which comes from one without love is dead.* The Holy Spirit is grieved by actions and attitudes which do not result in building others up according to their needs (Eph 4:29-30). Without the leading of the Spirit there is no assurance of praying according to God's will. And *no* prayer is answered which is not in harmony with God's will (1 Jn 5:14). You can have no positive experience of Christian prayer without Christian love. We pray to God, who *is* love.

Part of the reason why love is so important in the Christian community lies at the very heart of our redemption. When Christ died, he not only reconciled us to God, but also reconciled us to one another. Paul explains this in Ephesians 2, using the hostility between Jew and Gentile as the starting point. He explains that Christ's "purpose was to create in himself one new man out of the two, thus making peace, and in this one body to reconcile both of them to God through the cross, by which he put to death their hostility" (vv. 15-16). Later Paul explains that in the body of Christ, believers "are being *built together* to become a dwelling in which God lives by his Spirit" (v. 22). Thus the Christian community is a community of love and unity. Christ died to make peace, to reconcile and to put to death interpersonal hostility.

Paul saw the expression of love and unity as central to Christian worship. In the early church the Lord's Supper was celebrated with a communal meal known as the *agape*, or love feast (from the Greek word for self-giving Christian love). The service was a remembrance of Christ's death and the communion which resulted from it—communion between God and man *and* among people. These two themes come into focus as Paul speaks of the elements of Holy Communion:

> Is not the cup of thanksgiving for which we give thanks a participation in the blood of Christ? And is not the bread that we break a participation in the body of Christ? Because there is one loaf, we, who are many, are one body, for we all partake of the one loaf. (1 Cor 10:16-17)

Though evidence about the agape feast is sparse, it seems that various members of the Christian community brought what they could to be shared in a fellowship meal. When all had arrived the meal started. During the feast—perhaps near its end—wine and bread would be passed to commemorate Jesus' sacrificial love.[1] The agape feast embodied the truth that men and women of all races, socioeconomic strata and nations had been made one and reconciled to God through the cross. Though modern-day communion services tend to focus almost exclusively on Christ's sacrifice and refer to the bread as a symbol for Christ's physical body, it appears that the early church made a great deal of the bread as a symbol of Christ's spiritual body, the church, the loving communion of saints made possible by Christ's death.

In 1 Corinthians Paul harshly criticizes the church because the joyful demonstration of Christian love and unity in the agape feast was being turned into an ugly monument to social and economic differences. Paul explodes:

> When you come together, it is *not* the Lord's Supper you eat, for as you eat, each of you goes ahead without waiting for anybody else. One remains hungry, another gets drunk. . . . Do you *despise* the church of God and *humiliate* those who have nothing? (11:20-22)

Peter makes the connection between loving actions and prayer in marriage. He reminds Christian husbands of the spiritual equality of men and women in Christ and encourages them not to lord it over their wives but to sacrificially love them:

> Husbands, in the same way be considerate as you live with your wives, and treat them with respect as the [physically] weaker partner and as heirs with you of the gracious gift of life, so that nothing will hinder your prayers. (1 Pet 3:7)

The Amplified Bible renders the last phrase, "in order that your prayers may not be hindered *and* cut off. Otherwise you cannot pray effectively."[2] To fail to love others displeases God and breaks Christ's command. Those who would pray effectively can never afford to forget that we "receive from him anything we ask, because we obey his commands and do what pleases him. And this is his command: to believe in the name of his Son, Jesus Christ, and to love one another as he commanded us" (1 Jn 3:22-23).

So What Should I Do?

We are to love. Christ calls us to respond to the needs of others *as an expression of thanksgiving to God* for loving us. We are to love others for all they're worth. Being made in God's image and having Christ die for them indicates that people are worth a tremendous amount—no matter how wretched their existence or how sordid their sins. Christian love is patterned on God's love. He loved us (thought we were worth the sacrifice of his Son's life) even though we were unworthy. Thus Christian love is not based on the merit of its object. Nor does it grow in anticipation of any return benefits for the lover. Christian love sees others as inherently valuable and consequently nourishes, carefully protects and cherishes them (Eph 5:29). Christian love bears with the failings of the weak and seeks to build up others (Rom 15:2-3). Such behavior is *not* easy.

The command to love like Christ loves is a call for radical self-sacrifice. Jesus sharply underscored its difference from natural affection and self-serving kindness:

If you love those who love you, what credit is that to you? Even "sinners" love those who love them. And if you do good to those who are good to you, what credit is that to you? Even "sinners" do that. And if you lend to those from whom you expect repayment, what credit is that to you? Even "sinners" lend to "sinners," expecting to be repaid in full. But love your enemies, do good to them, and lend to them without expecting to get anything back. Then your reward will be great, and you will be sons of the Most High, because he is kind to the ungrateful and wicked. Be merciful, just as your Father is merciful. (Lk 6:32-36)

Given Jesus' attitude, it is not surprising that his disciples view the practical expression of love as the test of authentic faith (see, for example, 1 Jn 3:17-18; Jas 1:22; 2:14-16). And like true faith, practical love is also connected *directly* with prayer. Proverbs 21:13 affirms, "If a man shuts his ears to the cry of the poor, he too will cry out [to God] and not be answered." Such love goes against human instinct but is characteristic of those who are God's spiritual children.

You have heard that it was said, "Love your neighbor and hate your enemy." But I tell you: Love your enemies and pray for those who persecute you, that you may be sons of your Father in heaven. He causes his sun to rise on the evil and the good, and sends rain on the righteous and the unrighteous. (Mt 5:43-45)

Intercession

Love and prayer are connected in that loving others is something we do out of obedience to Christ's commands, and obedience is a prerequisite for effective prayer. But love and prayer also interrelate in that prayer is one way to love others. If I can do nothing else, I can pray for people. I can ask God to help others when I cannot. Prayer must never be a justification for failing to help others. Yet some circumstances are out of our hands, and only God knows how help should be given. In these situations we can do nothing but pray.

The scope of Christian intercession is as broad as the horizon of God's love: "I urge, then, first of all, that requests, prayers, intercession and thanksgiving be made for everyone—for kings and all those in authority, that we may live peaceful and quiet lives in all godliness and holiness" (1 Tim 2:1-2). Make intercessory prayer for others a regular part of your prayer experience. Pray for their needs. Make a list to focus your mind, be specific and systematic, and when possible follow up to learn of the Lord's response. Many people miss blessings in answered prayer simply because they pray only for themselves.

Pray for others because you love them and desire to do what is good and pleases God. Samuel reportedly said, "As for me, far be it from me that I should sin against the LORD by failing to pray for you" (1 Sam 12:23). He said this as one who functioned as prophet and priest in Israel. We tend to think of the priest's work in terms of the sacrificial ritual, but intercession was an important part of priestly ministry. Since Christians are not Old Testament priests like Samuel, failure to intercede is not the same kind of sin. The verse is misused if applied directly to Christians. However, not praying for others might be construed as sin on other grounds: (1) it falls within the scope of James 4:17: "Anyone, then, who knows the good he ought to do and doesn't do it, sins"; (2) 1 Timothy 2:1 is a command, as is James 5:16, to "pray for each other"; (3) through Jesus, the great High Priest, New Testament believers have been made "a royal priesthood" (1 Pet 2:9), a fact mentioned five times in the New Testament. Since Jesus now "lives to make intercession" according to Hebrews 7:25 (RSV; see also Rom 8:34), we may conclude that prayer for others is a responsibility which attaches to the priesthood of all believers.

Paul called believers to "be imitators of God, therefore, as dearly loved children and live a life of love, just as Christ loved us and gave himself up for us as a fragrant offering and sacrifice to God" (Eph 5:1-2).

Questions for Thought and Discussion

1. What do you think of the statement that we love God by loving other people? Is there *more* to loving God than loving other people?

2. Early church tradition says that in his old age the apostle John's message was reduced to "Little children, love one another." Assuming this to be historically accurate, why do you think he would have preached this way?

3. How do you think love and prayer are related?

4. How should we pray for our enemies? Is Luke 23:34 an example of this?

5. In a letter written in 1940 C. S. Lewis said:

When you pray for Hitler and Stalin how do you actually teach yourself to make the prayer real? The two things that help me are (a) A continual grasp of the idea that one is joining one's feeble voice to the perpetual intercession of Christ who died for these very men. (b) A recollection, as firm as I can make it, of all one's own cruelty; which might have blossomed under different conditions into something terrible. You and I are not at bottom so different from these ghastly creatures.[3]

Could you have prayed for Hitler or Stalin? Who do you today find it most difficult to pray for (an unjust leader, a personal enemy, etc.)?

6. What do you feel inside when someone says, "Please pray for me"? Can you be a Christian and answer no? Is it Christian to reply, "I will for two weeks"?

7. Are you ever afraid to ask others for prayer for yourself? Why or why not?

11
Forgiving: The Prayer for Other Sinners

You won't catch me getting ulcers," a man is said to have boasted. "For one thing, I just take life as it comes. For another, I don't ever hold a grudge, not even against people who did things to me that I'll *never* forgive!"

More than a few Christians think like this—perhaps because forgiving others is so hard and because the Bible treats the subject so seriously. But forgiveness is a topic we can't avoid in a book like this. Beyond question, Jesus intimately linked forgiving others with our effectiveness in prayer.

Forgiveness: The Bible Message
"Who can forgive sins but God alone?" This question was asked by

some Pharisees who had heard Jesus forgive the sins of a paralytic (Mk 2:7). The question expresses the conviction that the right of judgment (and hence, forgiveness) belongs to God alone. The idea that forgiveness is an attribute of divinity has deep roots in the Old Testament. It begins as early as God's self-description to Moses: "The LORD, the LORD, the compassionate and gracious God, slow to anger, abounding in love and faithfulness, maintaining love to thousands, and forgiving wickedness, rebellion and sin" (Ex 34:6-7). Later the psalmist proclaimed: "With you there is forgiveness; therefore you are feared" (130:4). Before the exile Isaiah gave as the word of the Lord, "I, even I, am he who blots out your transgressions, for my own sake, and remembers your sins no more" (43:25). During the nation's exile, Daniel prayed, "The Lord our God is merciful and *forgiving*, even though we have rebelled against him" (9:9). The Jews well understood the spiritual reality behind our popular aphorism: To err is human; but to forgive, divine.

Jesus is the embodiment of God's forgiveness. The Son of Man came "to serve, and to give his life as a ransom for many" (Mk 10:45). The Christian gospel is fundamentally a message of forgiveness. The apostles preached "repentance and forgiveness of sins . . . in his name to all nations" (Lk 24:47). Peter's message can be distilled down to "Everyone who believes in him receives forgiveness of sins through his name" (Acts 10:43). Experiencing God's forgiveness is an essential characteristic of God's people in *both* the old and new covenant eras.

The Forgiven Forgive
Because we as God's people have been forgiven, Christ also asks us to forgive others. Paul wrote: "Bear with each other and forgive whatever grievances you may have against one another. Forgive as the Lord forgave you" (Col 3:13).

Our primary motivation for forgiving others is gratitude for God's gift of forgiveness to us. We who have been liberated from the bondage and poverty of sin and made rich and free through God's grace should never be insensitive to similar needs in others.

And in forgiving others we follow the example of God, our Father: "Be merciful, just as your Father is merciful" (Lk 6:36). *Showing* mercy becomes a sign that one has received God's mercy in forgiveness. Our willingness to forgive others is thus a sign of our genuine conversion. Those who are unwilling to forgive cannot be viewed as God's children. Jesus regarded callous indifference to another's need for forgiveness as an ingratitude of such monstrous proportion that it was a blasphemous insult to God. The strength of his conviction is obvious in the parable of the unmerciful servant in Matthew 18.

In the parable Jesus described a man who had been forgiven an immense debt by his master. But the callous fellow was unmoved by his master's mercy. He went to another slave who owed him a small debt and had him thrown into debtors' prison because he could not make payment. The master heard about the situation from others in the household.

Then the master called the servant in. "You wicked servant," he said, "I canceled all that debt of yours because you begged me to. Shouldn't you have had mercy on your fellow servant just as I had on you?" In anger his master turned him over to the jailers until he should pay back all he owed. (Mt 18:32-34)

Jesus concludes by noting that "this is how my heavenly Father will treat each of you unless you forgive your brother from your heart" (v. 35). Why is this last line so severe? We can reasonably suppose that our Lord did not think we would find it easy to forgive others. Forgiveness requires that we be honest about our own shortcomings while valuing the one who has sinned against us. We naturally enjoy just the opposite: ignoring our own shortcomings by emphasizing our importance while focusing on the unworthiness of the one who has offended. "They can't do that to *me*!" comes naturally. "What they've done is evidence that they are hurting," does not. "How can I help this person get restored to fellowship with God?" is hard. "It'll be a snowy day in Ecuador before I forget what you did to me," is effortless.

Withholding forgiveness seems to give us power over another; it increases our feelings of importance. Forgiving acknowledges that before God *all* men and women are powerless and unworthy. Our real importance and value are most clearly demonstrated in God's act of forgiving us. What God has done for us in Christ is to say through his forgivenes that we are valuable, individually important—even when we sin. When we feel valued, recognition (through forgiveness) of another sinner's value (in spite of their unworthiness) is not threatening to our own self-esteem. By forgiving us God has given us the resource we need to forgive others.

The last line of Jesus' parable is not just a threat that the unmerciful may stop experiencing God's blessing. (Please note: the parable does *not* teach the loss of salvation. The master did not sell but jailed the servant.) It is primarily a powerful illustration of the "reciprocal spiritual principle." Jesus stated this more fully in Luke 6:37-38:

> Do not judge, and you will not be judged. Do not condemn, and you will not be condemned. Forgive, and you will be forgiven. Give, and it will be given to you. A good measure, pressed down, shaken together and running over, will be poured into your lap. For with the measure you use, it will be measured to you.

He restated this axiom at the conclusion of the Lord's Prayer in Matthew 6:14-15: "For if you forgive men when they sin against you, your heavenly Father will also forgive you. But if you do not forgive men their sins, your Father will not forgive your sins."

Jesus *assumes* that the forgiven sinner forgives others. Acts of forgiveness *identify* the petitioner as God's child, one who knows God's forgiveness and who has the right to come for daily cleansing on the basis of Christ's blood (1 Jn 1:9). In this context, Matthew 6:14 is *assurance* of ongoing, forgiveness for the forgiving child of God. Conversely Matthew 6:15 asserts that those who are not God's children—who do not forgive—cannot expect forgiveness.

But Surely There's a Limit

Being a forgiver is one thing. But being a whipping post is another. Peter may have been thinking along these lines when he asked, "Lord, how many times shall I forgive my brother when he sins against me? Up to seven times?" (Mt 18:21). Seven was used in Judaism to designate completeness, and so Peter's question might be paraphrased, "Surely seven is the limit, and a generous one at that."

Jesus' response was, "I do not say to you, up to seven times, but up to seventy times seven" (18:22 NASB). Seventy times seven (or perhaps "seventy-seven" as in NIV) can be taken to mean, "Have you stopped needing to be forgiven by God, Peter? Would you like him to stop forgiving you at seven? Of course not. Treat your brother the way God treats you. Forget about keeping track."

But given the Christian's willingness to forgive, isn't it possible to be taken advantage of? The answer is yes. But being rich in Christ, we are not bankrupted by others. We are still to "be patient, bearing with one another in love" (Eph 4:2).

This does not mean, however, that we are to completely ignore wrongs done to us. Specific instruction for cases when one Christian wrongs another is found in Matthew 18:15: "If your brother sins against you, go and show him his fault, just between the two of you. If he listens to you, you have won your brother." But a brother or sister's fault must be sin, a transgression of God's Word, not merely insensitivity to your personal preferences. You cannot rebuke a brother for feeling that free enterprise oppresses the poor or for wearing jeans to your dinner party, nor a sister for thinking natural foods are a rip-off, or for wanting to be an investment banker. But where there is sin, Christian love rebukes. And when one Christian shows another such a fault in love, the response should be to admit and confess the wrong, feeling genuine sorrow for the hurt and sin.[1] In some cases restitution for physical loss will be in order and in many cases it will take time to repair the relationship. But when sin is acknowledged and repented of by the guilty party, there *must* be forgiveness by the injured party.

The process was sketched by Jesus in Luke 17:3-4: "If your brother sins, rebuke him, and if he repents, forgive him. If he sins against you seven times in a day, and seven times comes back to you and says, 'I repent,' forgive him." The goal in this is "winning" your brother or sister, seeing them restored to fellowship with you, the church and with God. It is not to see them admit that you are right, and they are wrong. Nor is it to get them to admit an offense against your dignity. "Brothers, if someone is caught in a sin, you who are spiritual should *restore* him gently." But rebuke carries its own spiritual risk: doing it can set you up to feel self-righteous. "But watch yourself, or you also may be tempted" (Gal 6:1).

Yet even if the person *refuses* to repent, we are still to show love to that person. We are commanded not to repay anyone evil for evil nor to take revenge (Rom 12:17, 19). Paul says, " 'If your enemy is hungry, feed him; if he is thirsty, give him something to drink. In doing this, you will heap burning coals on his head.' Do not be overcome by evil, but overcome evil with good" (Rom 12:20-21). (The reference to burning coals here is probably an idiom for repentance—"the burning pangs of shame and contrition.")[2]

According to Jesus, we must also "pray for those who mistreat you" (Lk 6:28). But such injunctions are not intended to make fall guys or easy marks of Christians, as Paul's advice to Timothy clearly shows: "Alexander the metalworker did me a great deal of harm. The Lord will repay him for what he has done. You too should be on your guard against him, because he strongly opposed our message" (2 Tim 4:14-15).

Jesus' instruction in Matthew 18:16-17 is just as realistic. He knows that even Christians will reject rebuke:

> But if he will not listen, take one or two others along, so that "every matter may be established by the testimony of two or three witnesses." If he refuses to listen to them, tell it to the church; and if he refuses to listen even to the church, treat him as you would a pagan or a tax collector [an idiom for a hardened sinner].

Such excommunication is not retribution; it is discipline aimed at restoration. It is undertaken to get the errant Christian to see the severity of the sin and seek forgiveness and reconciliation.[3] The reasons for such action are three: to bring sinners to their senses and effect reconciliation, to protect the purity of others in the church, and to protect the witness of the church to nonbelievers.[4]

Jesus' Promise

Because of the seriousness of such situations, Jesus promised church leaders that he would guide them in making decisions: "Where two or three come together in my name, there am I with them" (Mt 18:20). It is *not* at all certain that this promise has universal applicability to all Christian meetings. Paul's parallel wording in 1 Corinthians 5:4 suggests that he knew these words of Jesus and took them to refer to disciplinary situations. The agreement spoken of in Matthew 18:19 ("Again, I tell you that if two of you on earth agree about anything you ask for, it will be done for you by my Father in heaven") is likely to refer to prayer for guidance and wisdom before taking drastic disciplinary action. This verse, too, is often used out of context. Certainly it does *not* affirm that agreement by two Christians who pray will guarantee God's response to that prayer. In Matthew 18 the Lord's assurance is that in situations involving discipline, when the mind of God is sought, those asking for help in prayer will be given his help. They may proceed in faith that the person who rejects the offer of forgiveness by refusing to repent will be bound to the consequences of that sin, both in heaven and on earth; and that those who accept rebuke and through repentance seek reconciliation will be loosed from their sin by the forgiveness of the church and God. "I tell you the truth, whatever you bind on earth will be bound in heaven, and whatever you loose on earth will be loosed in heaven" (Mt 18:18).[5]

The importance of both seeking and giving forgiveness among Christians cannot be ignored. Hostility and an unforgiving spirit are acids which destroy our capacity to worship and pray. When sin and discord exist between Christians, God is troubled. And Scripture indicates that hostility between believers hinders acceptable praise and worship. Jesus remarks in the Sermon on the Mount,

> Therefore, if you are offering your gift at the altar and there remember that your brother has something against you, leave your gift there in front of the altar. First go and be reconciled

to your brother; then come and offer your gift. (Mt 5:23-24)
Jesus' words mean that interpersonal reconciliation must be placed
before worship. He implies that worship offered in the face of a
known need for reconciliation is unacceptable to God. The Spirit of
love and unity is *grieved* by hostility between those whom Christ
died to reconcile: "And do not grieve the Holy Spirit of God with
whom you were sealed for the day of redemption. Get rid of all
bitterness, rage and anger, brawling and slander, along with every
form of malice" (Eph 4:30-31).

By what sleight of hand do we expect an omniscient Jesus, who
knows our thoughts, to ignore hostility between us—which he died
to end? For our worship to be acceptable, we must "be kind and
compassionate to one another, forgiving each other, just as in
Christ God forgave you" (Eph 4:31).

Forgiveness and Prayer

Jesus' words in Mark 11:25 directly connect personal prayer and
forgiving: "And when you stand praying, if you hold anything
against anyone, forgive him, so that your Father in heaven may
forgive your sins." The implication is that an unforgiving spirit
hinders prayer.[6]

David directly connected God's blessing with unity among his
people: "How good and pleasant it is when brothers live together
in unity. . . . For there the LORD bestows his blessing" (Ps 133:1,
3). The writer of Proverbs also puts "hatred" among the things
which "are detestable to" God. This includes "a man who stirs up
dissension among brothers" (Prov 6:16, 19). We are commanded to
forgive. Harboring an unforgiving spirit is sin. And God does not
hear those who cherish sin (Ps 66:18). It all goes back to the relationship between prayer and obedience. If we obey, we grow to
know the mind of God and we will begin to pray according to his
will. Such prayers are answered. But if we do not forgive, we do
not obey and we grow distant from God. We will thus have trouble
knowing his will and praying according to it.

Thankfully, our God is a loving and forgiving Father—even when his children are neither. I've said what I have in the last two chapters to motivate you to love and to encourage you to forgive. My purpose is not to crush or accuse. God hears the prayers of those who struggle to do his will. If you have been unloving or know you should seek reconciliation or grant forgiveness, ask him for the Spirit's help, and by faith try to be obedient to his Word. It is not easy. But the freedom and liberty which comes in worship and prayer when we get rid of such clutter in our spiritual lives is definitely worth the cost.

Questions for Thought and Discussion

1. Why do we want people to admit that they have wronged us?
2. Why does God want us to admit it when we have wronged him?
3. How does the parable of the unmerciful servant (Mt 18:21-25) relate to Christian life today? What sort of debts do we have to other people? You couldn't run a business and forgive all your debts. Why does Jesus make such an extreme demand of his followers?
4. Is forgiveness really as personally expensive as the author says it is?
5. What does it mean to forgive and forget?
6. How do you think an unforgiving spirit might interfere with your prayers?

12
Believing: The Prayer of Faith

One day I heard my daughter, Hillery, make an interesting remark to a little friend: "Don't worry; my Daddy can fix anything."

The faith of a five-year-old burns bright. But I found myself wondering, "Will she have the same faith in her daddy when she realizes there are things he either cannot or will not fix?" That question raised even more serious ones: What does it mean to have faith in our heavenly Father? How much do we trust him when he chooses not to "fix" things? I *know* that nothing is too hard for the Lord. But it is difficult for me to have the faith of a child—even though I know Jesus loves me.

Personal and Objective Faith

Faith is very personal. But it also must be objectively definable, because faith is only as good as its object. Many of us have lost sight of this. Our age places an unbiblical emphasis on personal and subjective religious experiences. Our society treats religion as a wholly subjective experience—something "just between me and God." Many people feel that it doesn't matter so much *what* they believe as *that* they believe.

The roots of such thinking can be traced to existential or humanist philosqphies, but there is an element of truth in these ideas. We *are* all unique persons who must choose for ourselves. And Christ does mean something a little different to each of us. Yet Jesus claimed that it does matter in *whom* and *what* you believe.

Jesus claimed that he *alone* was the one true living way to God (Jn 14:6): "No one comes to the Father except through me." His apostles made similar claims. Peter's is typical: "Salvation is found in no one else, for there is no other name under heaven given to men by which we must be saved" (Acts 4:12). Paul was dogmatic about the relation between historical fact—particularly Jesus' resurrection—and the Christian faith: "If Christ has not been raised, your faith is *futile*" (1 Cor 15:17). In saying this he followed Jesus who also connected faith with reasonable objective evidence: "Reach here your finger, and see My hands; and reach here your hand, and put it into My side; and be not unbelieving, but believing" (Jn 20:27 NASB). Jesus' appeal here to Thomas shows us that personal faith is not a blind leap into the dark.

Nevertheless, Christians still confuse faith with irrationality. Hebrews 11:1 defines faith as "being sure of what we hope for and certain of what we do not see." And since many people never see their fondest hopes, faith seems akin to clinging to an impossible dream. A child defined faith as "believing what you know is impossible," and Tertullian once remarked during a discussion of the miraculous, "I believe it because it is absurd."[1] This kind of believing obviously takes effort, as Lewis Carroll's White Queen makes clear to Alice in *Through the Looking Glass:*"I can't believe *that!*" said Alice.

"Can't you?" the Queen said in a pitying tone. "Try again: draw a long breath, and shut your eyes."

Alice laughed. "There's no use trying," she said, "one *can't* believe impossible things."

"I daresay you haven't much practice," said the Queen. "When I was your age, I always did it for half-an-hour a day. Why, sometimes I've believed as many as six impossible things before breakfast."[2]

God does not desire that we believe something that goes against rationality, reality or history. When Jesus called the disciples "you of little faith" in Matthew 8:26, he was rebuking them for failing to take facts they already had to a logical conclusion. The miracles they had previously seen Jesus work provided reasonable evidence for them to believe he also had the power to protect them from the storm. This approach to faith is seen throughout the Bible. Faith is a rational response to the evidence of God's self-revelation in nature, human history, the Scriptures and his resurrected Son.

Faith Is Trust in God

But faith is *more* than the drawing of conclusions from facts. James explains that though they are implacably opposed to God's work, "the demons also believe" (2:19 NASB). Faith requires total personal commitment, the willingness to entrust the whole of one's being to God without reservation.

The true nature of faith is clarified when a believer faces death. This is evident in Jesus' prayer from the cross, "Father, into your hands I commit my spirit" (Lk 23:46). Stephen said in the pit of stoning, "Lord Jesus, receive my spirit" (Acts 7:59). At that moment trust must rest in God himself, in his character, his ability and the veracity of his promises, not whether the believer has enough faith.

At death human faith ends. Great faith that you can fly a hang glider counts for nearly nothing when you jump off the cliff. What matters is only whether the object of your faith—the design, structure and durability of your glider—is sound. No amount of pilot skill can compensate for a flawed craft. And so it is with faith at death.

You cannot fly through death to eternal life on the strength of your faith. The issue is whether you have entrusted yourself to Someone who can be trusted. To have faith in your faith, rather than in God, is a fatal mistake.

Both Jesus and Stephen faced death certain that their hope of resurrection to eternal life was well placed *in God*. Paul concurs: "I know *whom* I have believed, and am convinced that *he* is able to guard what I have entrusted to *him* for that day" (2 Tim 1:12).

Though we often speak of faith as something which men and women have or exercise, the New Testament regards faith as a gift which God graciously gives us because we cannot exercise it on our own. We are unable to obey God's law or to respond to the gospel because our minds have been blinded by Satan. We "are justified," Paul says, "freely by his grace through the redemption that came by Christ Jesus" (Rom 3:24). Salvation is appropriated, or received, through personal faith. But even faith is God's gift: "It is by grace you have been saved, through faith—and this not from yourselves, it is the gift of God" (Eph 2:8).[3]

The necessity for God to give faith to men and women because of our hostility, spiritual blindness and inability is plain enough. What is not so clear is how then the New Testament authors can exhort us to have faith. How can Paul hold that a man cannot see the light of the gospel of the glory of Christ, and yet tell the Philippian jailer, "Believe in the Lord Jesus, and you will be saved" (Acts 16:31). This difficulty is nowhere explained. But there can be no doubt human responsibility (to believe, exercise faith) and God's sovereignty (to give faith as a gift) are *both* taught in Scripture. The matter is an example of an antinomy, an interface of apparently contradictory truths which characterize the meeting of humanity and divinity. Both ideas must be affirmed if our thinking is to stay biblical. And if we are to think biblically about faith in relation to prayer, this paradox is inescapable.

Banking on Faith
I've stressed the role of God in faith because growing numbers of

Christians have been led to believe that faith is something they must generate themselves (almost out of nothing) if God is to respond to their prayers. They see faith as a commodity they exchange for answers to prayer. Christians talk as if faith were something God measures in centimeters or weighs in ounces. If you have enough you are heard. If you don't have enough right now, you can probably bank enough eventually through persistence (fasting adds six per cent a month), or get a loan from two or three others (who gather and agree on your behalf). There is, of course, always the possibility that you might convince some righteous man (one just full of faith) to offer some effective fervent intercession on your behalf. That kind has more faith than they need themselves.

For some, God has become an unscrupulous commodities broker. They are chagrined because they *know* they had enough faith, yet God didn't bless them financially as he did the man they saw on TV. Others become critical of fellow believers in exuberance which follows blessing: "I can't help it if I have enough faith to be healed and she doesn't. Some of us do, but others don't." And more than a few get discouraged because they know they do not have enough faith to "make it work." In our day when answers to prayer are treated like rewards for faith, thousands of Christians are becoming disillusioned with the whole gospel because they can't get what they want out of God.

Hebrews 11:6 distills the content of faith in biblical religion (and hence Christian prayer) down to two essentials: "Without faith it is impossible to please him. For whoever would draw near to God must believe that he exists and that he rewards those who seek him" (RSV).

Drawing near to God in prayer requires: (1) belief in his existence; and (2) positive conviction about his moral character. The first seems straightforward. You cannot develop a relationship with somebody who doesn't exist. All Christians believe in God, don't they? But I don't think it's that simple. In modern society it is easy to intellectually assent to God's existence yet live life with no reference or dependence on God—except when disaster strikes. We live in a structured, regulated and double-indemnity insured and insulated way.

What does it matter if God sends the sun? Fluorescent lighting is more even; the sun causes skin cancer, and you can get tanned faster under the lights at the health club. God sends the rain, but we have umbrellas, flood-control systems, domed stadiums, shopping malls and indoor tennis courts. God controls the seasons and the agricultural cycles, but we have subsidies and price supports, frozen peas, nitrogen-fixed apples, dehydrated beefsteaks and sugarless gum. God has appointed man once to die, but we have group health insurance, trauma centers, intensive-care units, chromium-alloy burial vaults and perpetual-care interment. Maybe there's a place for God in Mecca or Jerusalem, but the rest of us are too busy to give it much thought.

Only when the routine is disturbed by illness, bankruptcy or war does the need for God's existence seep back into our consciousness. Although we have no intention of actually suppressing the knowledge of God, our urban life just seems to make God unnecessary. You have to believe *against* the grain of modern life, and it takes effort—especially if you are a city dweller—just to remain conscious that God exists, let alone find time to pray to him.

To know *that* God exists, however, is only the first aspect of biblical faith. The second aspect is a positive conviction about God's moral character. As I said earlier, your belief that you can work a hang glider is not as important as the quality of the glider. We may be able to believe God exists, but the important thing is who God is. Praying in faith assumes having access to data about God. Information concerning what God is like is available from three sources: (1) his creation—the evidence of nature, order, design, beauty and so on; (2) his creatures—human nature and testimony, human history; and (3) his self-revelation in Scripture.

Since the evidence of nature has been defaced through human sin (Gen 3:17; Rom 8:20) and even redeemed human nature suffers from sin (Rom 5:12-13; 7:21-22), our most certain source of information about God is his written Word, the Bible.

I do not want to discourage study of the faith and prayer experiences of other Christians such as George Müller. But if you forget that Müller was an avid student of the Bible and attempt to develop faith like his without your own regular reading of Scripture, you will get quite frustrated. Faith, the ability to trust God, is like a plant. It takes time to grow and requires consistent exposure to the light of God's Word.

Who Is God?

What are the key characteristics of God which relate to prayers of faith? We've already looked at several of them, so we can just summarize here. First, we must believe in God's *omnipotence*. It makes no sense to ask for things which are beyond another's ability to accomplish or deliver. God's power is not merely his ability to work with or through circumstances as they presently are. He retains the creative abilities which called the world into existence: "By faith we understand that the universe was formed at God's command" (Heb 11:3). Faith in God's almighty creative power is the first thing mentioned in one of Jeremiah's prayers: "Ah, Sovereign LORD, you have made the heavens and the earth by your great power and outstretched arm. Nothing is too hard for you" (Jer 32:17).

But it does not follow—as so many seem to think—from faith in God's omnipotence that anything can happen in response to prayer. Our omnipotent God does *not* give us through prayer a blank check which can be cashed for anything if we have sufficient faith. Faith must be placed in God, God as he is described in the Bible, not in the fertility and strength of our powers of imagination. So-called possibility praying, which appeals to Mark 9:23 ("everything is possible for him who believes") for support but ignores the rest of Scripture, can seem fantastic, but unfortunately it is only slightly removed from fantasizing. What you believe is possible *must* be informed, controlled and circumscribed by what God has revealed about himself and his promises in Scripture.

So what does God promise? How ought our prayers to be conditioned? Abraham's faith in God's omnipotence was conditioned by knowledge of God's Word. Since God had *specifically* promised that he and Sarah would have a child, Abraham's faith was the conviction that God would act. Given such a promise, to doubt would impugn either the Lord's ability or his integrity. However, God did not explain initially either how or when the child would be born, and waiting was not easy, as the account in Genesis shows. Abraham's case illustrates a major precept concerning what it means to pray in faith: *Faith must be absolute that God will respond to prayer if he has specifically and unconditionally promised to do so.*

John tells us, "If we confess our sins, he is faithful and just and will forgive us our sins and purify us from all unrighteousness" (1 Jn 1:9). Because we have that promise, we slur God's trustworthiness and justice if we confess and pray for cleansing and then subsequently feel that our sin was not forgiven.

James tells us, "If any of you lacks wisdom, he should ask God, who gives generously to all without finding fault, and it will be given to him" (Jas 1:5). Claiming this promise in prayer must be accompanied by the conviction and certainty that God will grant wisdom. Still, the promise does not specify how or when God may remedy the deficiency, and so faith must be patient. In fact, the verses which precede this promise suggest that wisdom may come through trials and testing. In relation to this specific promise James goes on to say,

But when he asks, he must believe and not doubt, because he who doubts is like a wave of the sea, blown and tossed by the wind. That man should not think he will receive anything from the Lord; he is a double-minded man, unstable in all he does. (Jas 1:6-8)

The seriousness of doubt (which means "unbelief") in this case is that it disparages God's character and discredits his generosity in promising wisdom to those who ask for it.

These promises for wisdom and forgiveness both are grounded in the moral character of God. And this is the emphasis in the

second item mentioned in Hebrews 11:6. In addition to belief that
God exists, that he has the power to answer prayer and that he
has promised to answer prayer, we must also believe "that he
rewards those who earnestly seek him." The concept that God
rewards means that God's response to prayer is always benevolent,
that he is willing to meet our needs in the best possible way. David
put it like this:

The LORD is gracious and compassionate,

slow to anger and rich in love.

The LORD is good to all;

he has compassion on all he has made. (Ps 145:8-9)

Jesus illustrated this principle in the context of family relationships:

Which of you, if his son asks for bread, will give him a stone?
Or if he asks for a fish, will give him a snake? If you, then,
though you are evil, know how to give good gifts to your children, how much more will your Father in heaven give good gifts
to those who ask him! (Mt 7:9-11)

We cannot overemphasize the importance of the conviction that
God's character is wholly good, gracious and compassionate. Why
is this conviction so important? Because *faith trusts in God rather than
insisting on its own way.* Such faith is certain that God always responds
with goodness and wisdom when our prayers are consistent with
God's will but are not based on specific promises in Scripture. This
kind of faith, as Bishop B. F. Westcott said, results in "not so much
the granting of a specific petition, which is assumed by the petitioner to be the way to the end desired, but the assurance that what
is granted does most effectively lead to that end."[4]

Since there are few generally applicable yet specific promises in
Scripture, most of our prayers must be offered in accordance with
this principle. This does not mean that our prayers must become
hesitant and tentative ("Do you suppose, Father, that maybe it
would be all right if . . .") or that they should be peppered with "if
it be thy will." Saying humble words is not the issue; what matters
is the attitude of the petitioner. Before you pray, examine the Scrip-

tures on the topic—use a concordance and Bible dictionary if necessary. Seek the wisdom of mature believers, and ask the Spirit to help you evaluate your motives. If your desire seems within the will of God, then trust God to bring it to pass. Commit yourself to him wholeheartedly. Pray with fervency and urgency. All requests within the scope of God's will are granted . . . in God's way and at the best possible time. Wait on God expectantly.

Should it become clear that God does not feel it is best to respond as you have prayed, then *continue to trust in God.* Thank him for caring enough about you to say no. If you feel like taking your marbles and going home alone, it may be that you are fatigued, perhaps stretched emotionally. Perhaps you have not really prayed with faith in God. Did you trust in a loving, wise and good Father at the height of his powers, or has it seemed that you have to wrest your desires from the stingy hand of a senile old fuddy-duddy who doesn't know what is best for you?

No matter what you are feeling about God, *keep on talking.* Tell him how you feel when he says no. Tell him it hurts, that you thought you understood his will, that disappointment is crushing. Tell him it is hard to trust either him or yourself right now. Ask him to restore your soul, to protect it from bitterness. Ask him to keep you from the tempter's invitation to anger and hostility. Ask him to search your heart, to cleanse you from selfishness and self-pity. Ask him to give you back the joy of your salvation. Thank him for your salvation. Thank him for loving you enough to die for you. Tell him that you want to trust him, and ask him to help you with your disappointment.

Seen from the viewpoint of faith, unanswered petition is not evidence that God isn't there, that he doesn't care or even that there is something wrong with your prayer. It illustrates the fact that the children of God do not always see things the way their Father does. Rather than falling into the void of disappointed nothingness, they are able to sink unashamedly into the loving arms of God.

Paul told the Romans, "God . . . is my witness how constantly I remember you in my prayers at all times; and I pray that now at last *by God's will* the way may be opened for me to come to you" (Rom 1:9-10). His confidence in the wisdom and goodness of God allowed him to pursue his ministry wholeheartedly even though he knew the disappointment of unanswered prayer: "I planned many times to come to you (but have been prevented from doing so until now)" (1:13). Daniel's three friends had a similar conviction: God can be trusted . . . even if we *die* with a prayer for deliverance on our lips.

Shadrach, Meshach and Abednego replied to the king, "O Nebuchadnezzar, we do not need to defend ourselves before you in this matter. If we are thrown into the blazing furnace, the God we serve is able to save us from it, and he will rescue us from your hand, O king. But even if he does not, we want you to know, O king, that we will not serve your gods or worship the image of gold you have set up." (Dan 3:16-18)

These men wanted to be delivered from the fire and their faith was certain that God had the power to do so. But having no specific promise that faithfulness to God would ensure their lives, they put their faith in God rather than in their ability to discern his will. This kind of faith in God's goodness and wisdom prays, "if it be thy will," not as a psychological hedge against disappointment but in realistic recognition of the difference between creatures and their Creator. Where there is no specific promise in Scripture, faith trusts not in itself but in God himself.[5]

Faith in Faith vs. Faith in God

The difficulties inherent in praying with *faith in your faith* are illustrated by the results of prayer when God says no. This approach to prayer is essentially an attempt to use a system to obtain a desired result. God is important. He powers the system. But faith becomes more important. It permits God to work. The goal is getting the answer. When the answer is not forthcoming, we are left only with questions: Did I have enough faith? Did my friends who prayed with me have enough faith? Should I have fasted or perhaps claimed a different promise? Attention is centered on prayer methods and techniques for generating faith. Thoughts center on us. Then they begin to shift with measurable envy toward those who apparently had enough faith: Why him or her and not me? The progression may end in speculations about the reality of God's love, justice and goodness. The result? We feel alienated from ourselves: we have too little faith. We feel alienated from others: they had enough faith. And we feel alienated from God who set up such a system in the first place. Essentially we are telling God how to glorify himself in our lives . . . and he wouldn't do it.

When we pray with faith *in God* and receive no answers, there are still questions, but there is also God. Prayer is seen as a means of communication between personal beings, and faith is an expression of commitment to the relationship. We are important, but God is more important—so we don't try to manipulate him by means of faith. The goal is to understand God, to know him better. When his response to prayer is no, such faith can still cling to God and waits to see him glorified his way through whatever answer is best for the relationship.

For those so committed to God the question Why? following unanswered prayer is still very real, but the answer is different: Because he loves me. This approach to prayer and faith allows us to appraise ourselves realistically. Since God said no, he feels our faith in him is strong enough to withstand the loss of that specific reinforcement. Second, no as an answer helps to reinforce our consciousness that God knows his children have different needs. He treats us differently because each of us *is* different: a unique combination of genes, experiences and abilities. Third, since God's no has not made us self-sufficient in the area of concern, we are drawn to others for encouragement and support. And this helps reinforce the fact that we need to be loved by one another. Fourth, we wait and wonder for him to show us how he will glorify himself in our life. The result? A more honest picture of ourselves, recognition that we need others, and anticipation of future growth in our relationship with God. It comes down to this: Faith in faith says, "Lord, I have the faith to get what I want: Lord, I need it." Faith in God says, "Lord, give me faith to accept what you want: Lord, I need you."

What Makes Faith Grow?

Faith is something Scripture says we need to pray effectively, and most of us wish we knew how to gain the faith which characterized the prayer lives of people such as George Müller, Hudson Taylor, Andrew Murray and Robert Murray McCheyne. Seeking secrets of faith, we read their biographies and imitate their devotions. Provided that this does not replace study of Scripture, I encourage you to research and reflect on the lives and prayers of the church's heroes of faith. Too many believers are unaware of the insights to be gained by reading about glorified Christians such as Polycarp, Clement of Rome, Augustine, Chrysostom, Basil, Anselm, Bernard of Clairvaux, Francis of Assisi, Thomas á Kempis, Tyndale, Luther, Calvin, Bunyan, William Law, Samuel Rutherford, the Scottish Covenanters, John Newton, William Wilberforce, Susannah Wesley, Praying Hyde, Rees Howard, D. L. Moody, Amanda Smith, C. T. Studd, Henry Ward Beecher, Mary Slessor, Dietrich Bonhoeffer, Helen Roseveare, A. W. Tozer and Corrie ten Boom. Ours is not the first generation to know God, and it is arrogant to think that the Spirit can teach us nothing through the godly counsel and experience of others.[6] One of the profound tragedies of modern Christianity is that so many believers know almost nothing about the saints of God in other denominations and communions or in ages other than their own.

But having said this, I must repeat again that faith is a gift from God, a fruit produced in us not so much by human effort as the power of the Holy Spirit. Because of this, when we find it hard to believe, we must ask God for help. To experience growth in trust we must follow the pattern in Luke 17:5 where "the apostles said to the Lord, 'Increase our faith.' " George Müller regarded his life as a demonstration of what God might do through the prayers of an *ordinary* Christian. Müller is said by some to have possessed the spiritual gift of faith mentioned in 1 Corinthians 12:9. But Müller personally claimed he did not have that gift.[7] That he regarded faith as a gift from God rather than something he could generate is evident in this statement from his diary:

This is, perhaps, of all days the most remarkable so far as regards the funds. When I was in prayer this morning respecting them, *I was enabled firmly to believe that the Lord would send help*, though all seemed dark as to natural circumstances.[8]

Müller went on to explain that a gift had been sent *before* he prayed. It was delivered while the Orphan House staff prayed again later in the day.

God will enable you, as he did Müller, to trust him for that which is in accordance with his will. His Spirit will give conviction that God will send help. The One who inhabits eternity has already done what you believe he will certainly do. This is the thought behind Jesus' words in Mark 11:24, "All things for which you pray and ask, believe that you have received them, and they shall be granted you" (NASB). It also is the basis for John's statement in 1 John 5: "This is the assurance we have in approaching God: that if we ask anything according to his will, he hears us. And if we know that he hears us—whatever we ask—we know that we have what we asked of him" (vv. 14-15).

If you choose, on the basis of such verses, to thank God before actually holding the answer to your prayer in your hand, be careful that your thanksgiving is merely that. Thanking God in advance can become an attempt at psychological leverage which subtly but plainly says: "Stand Thou and deliver! And do it soon, or else You're not all You've promised to be."

Faith and Risk

Müller's diary says that after praying with the staff for funds, he merely told them, "God will surely send help." Whether he thanked God in advance is not stated. What does become clear is that Müller often acted after prayer in a manner which could be called an obedience of faith. He is known to have taken risks—from the viewpoint of human and natural circumstances—because of faith that

God was going to respond to need. On one occasion the Orphan House children were actually brought to the table for a meal when there was no food. Müller did this not to force God's hand, but because he had been given faith through prayer that God would provide. By faith he saw the power, wisdom and trustworthiness of him who is invisible and acted rationally and responsibly on the basis of what he saw. Müller did not call a press conference or tell the staff to stand by for a miracle. He simply told them there was no need to worry.

God will help you, as he has countless persons, to learn to trust and obey.

I have come to think that prayer results in growth in faith when there is something at risk. Repeatedly in both Scripture and Christian history I have found that God is willing to encourage faith through answered prayer in those who *by doing his will* have found themselves confronting some kind of risk. These risks are rarely created by the petitioner but occur as the believer follows a path of obedience to God's Word. Consider the great cloud of witnesses mentioned in Hebrews 11:32-38:

Gideon, Barak, Samson, Jephthah, David, Samuel and the prophets, who through faith conquered kingdoms, administered justice, and gained what was promised; who shut the mouths of lions, quenched the fury of the flames, and escaped the edge of the sword; whose weakness was turned to strength; and who became powerful in battle and routed foreign armies. . . . Some faced jeers and flogging, while still others were chained and put in prison. They were stoned; they were sawed in two; they were put to death by the sword. They went about in sheepskins and goatskins, destitute, persecuted and mistreated—the world was not worthy of them. They wandered in deserts and mountains, and [lived] in caves and holes in the ground.

Reading this I wonder, how often are we *unwilling* to follow God's will into situations which are neither safe, comfortable, familiar, regulated, scheduled nor routine? Is it this which keeps us from opportunities of risk where we might receive through prayer faith to trust God to do what our training, skill and strength cannot? I think so. But what can we *do* to increase our faith? It seems to come down to obedience, the willingness to respond when the Holy Spirit says, "This is the way, walk in it." This is risky business, both before and following prayer. But it is the way of faith.

Does Faith Mean Speedy Answers?

The example cited from Müller's life is a case where God provided faith and the answer to the petition in close proximity. The answer was in his hand almost as soon as Müller got up off his knees. Yet Müller also knew about persistent prayer. He prayed for years, for example, for the salvation of two friends. But he never saw their conversion. These men were eventually saved—one at Müller's funeral and the other some months later.

Elijah—a man commended for praying in faith—told Ahab, "There is the sound of a heavy rain," even before he began to pray for rain (1 Kings 18:41). Earlier that day he received an instant answer when fire fell from heaven after his prayer. Yet despite God's specific promise, "I will send rain on the land" (1 Kings 18:1), Elijah had to pray repeatedly (seven times according to v. 43) before seeing evidence of God's coming answer.

God's delay in putting answers in our hands seems, in fact, to be a major way he encourages faith. Having seen that he is faithful following prayer over a week, you find it easier to trust him for ten days. Seeing the answer to persistence after a month strengthens me to wait in faith even longer for another. The implication of this—no matter how many instant answers God may be pleased to give along the way—is that Christians will never arrive at a faith plateau where they trust God just enough.

God will stretch our faith by letting us wait for answers both ordinary and extraordinary during the rest of our Christian life. This is true because it is impossible to trust him for too much: He "is able to do immeasurably more than all we ask or imagine" (Eph 3:20). And it is impossible to trust him for too long: "To him be glory in the church and in Christ Jesus throughout all generations, for ever and ever!" (v. 21). Just as we hunger and thirst for righteousness all our lives, so through the privilege of prayer God gives his Spirit the opportunity to make our appetite for greater commitment to him insatiable.

Patience and faith thus develop together in prayer. Poverty, persecution, suffering and imprisonment all seem to speed the process, because they reinforce awareness of dependence on God. But we who do not have such helps—who live in relative comfort in the world's instant-everything societies—must think against the grain of our hurried, impatient pushbutton existence if we are to think biblically about how God nurtures faith. As with nearly all living things, growing faith takes time.

Questions for Thought and Discussion

1. James 5:15 says, "The prayer offered in faith will make the sick person well; the Lord will raise him up." When an ill believer dies, even though a large number have prayed for healing, is the critical factor a lack of faith? Explain.

2. What is the difference between "faith in faith" and "faith in God"? Give examples of both.

3. Imagine that two believers both pray for healing from a chronic illness. One is healed and the other is not. What should the attitudes of the two be? What struggles will they face given God's differing answers to their prayers?

4. Some radio and television preachers assert that God wants his children to be prosperous. They urge Christians to pray, naming the blessing they desire and claiming it through faith as God's gift to them. What do you think about these "name it, claim it" approaches to prayer?

5. "Faith trusts in God rather than insisting on its own way." Do you agree or disagree with this view? Explain your answer.

6. How can you believe with all your heart that God will answer your prayer and yet not find your confidence in him shattered when he does not?

7. How does waiting for God to answer prayer encourage faith to grow?

8. Describe a time when there was risk involved in what you asked for or in your situation. Do you think praying in such situations is baiting or testing God?

13
Persisting: Doubt, Prayer and Fasting

One of the first things children learn—before they even learn to talk—is where we keep the cookies. At about one year of age, they learn that the cookies are in the kitchen, but somewhere up high, out of reach. Whenever they get hungry they go to the place, just below the cupboard, and stand with uplifted arms pleading, "Eh! Eh! Eh!" Because they are still very small, they must depend on (and convince) Mommy or Daddy to reach up to the special place and give them the goodies they want.

Hanging in There: Persistence and Importunity
Most of us think of persistent prayer in this way. And like the child's faith in a parent, persistent prayer is simply a matter of

having reasonable faith in God. It is reasonable to follow Jesus'
advice (Mt 7:7-8) and

- ☐ keep on asking—if God exists;
- ☐ keep on seeking—if God is all powerful and sovereign;
- ☐ keep on knocking—if God is wise and good and will give us what we need.

Far too often Christians talk as if reason were somehow a threat
to faith. But there are extremely few Christians who are actually
argued away from faith. And I suspect there are even fewer who
conclude on rational grounds that God has been *proven* to be unworthy of continued trust. For prayer which persists, we need "the
power to go on believing not in the teeth of reason but in the teeth
of lust, and terror and jealousy and boredom and indifference."[1]

Two things these days thwart persistent prayer. The first is our
time orientation. Persisting in prayer is not popular anymore because there isn't time to do it. Who can wait for God to get around
to responding? If you want to trust God for more than instant
answers, you may have to change the way you live. It's hard, very
hard, for Christians who are used to instant pudding, instant credit
and instant replay to wait for anything . . . even God.

The second complicating factor is misunderstanding. Persistence
and importunity are *not* methods we adopt to convince a reluctant
God that we are serious; nor must we pray long—through a period
of discipline—so we will appreciate the value of God's blessing.
Persistence often does provide a time of waiting during which we
can evaluate our motives and obtain the counsel of others. But we
persist in prayer primarily as an expression of our *complete dependency*
on God for all aspects of our existence. Persistence and importunity
affirm our recognition of the reality that apart from God we can
do nothing. Persistence flows from the certainty of our creaturely
helplessness and the logical conviction that God *alone* can help.
"Whom," says prayer persistence and importunity, "have I in heav-
en but you?" (Ps 73:25).

Persistence is an act of humility as well as an expression of faith.
This attitude is diametrically opposite the popular notion that if we

are importunate over a long enough period, God will eventually see the strength of our desire and respond. That is manipulation. It says, "Look at me; Look At Me; LOOK AT ME!" while humility says, "I'm looking to you; I'm looking to You; I'm looking to YOU." The point? Great faith in God *always* expresses itself in humble acknowledgment of dependency.

Consider two incidents when people petitioned Jesus. In the first, the Canaanite woman kept crying out to the Savior, "Lord, Son of David, have mercy on me! . . . Even the dogs eat the crumbs that fall from their masters' table" (Mt 15:22, 27).

Jesus' response was, "Woman, you have great faith! Your request is granted" (v. 28).

In the second instance the centurion said to Jesus, "Lord, don't trouble yourself, for I do not deserve to have you come under my roof. That is why I did not even consider myself worthy to come to you. But say the word, and my servant will be healed."

Jesus responded, "I tell you, I have not found such great faith even in Israel" (Lk 7:1-10).

Certainty that Jesus possessed power to heal (even from a distance) and confidence in his benevolence are aspects of faith. Both are examples of importunate persistence. Matthew 8:5 tells us the centurion came "beseeching" (RSV) or "entreating" (NASB), and Luke 7:4 tells us others also pleaded on his behalf. The woman's persistence actually bothered the disciples: "Send her away, for she keeps crying out after us" (Mt 15:23). Yet in both cases it is a statement of *humility* which is followed immediately by Jesus' words about great faith.

The attitudes which should characterize importunate persistence in prayer have been helpfully summed up by Peter: "God opposes the proud but gives grace to the humble. Humble yourselves, therefore, under God's mighty hand, that he may lift you up in due time. Cast all your anxiety on him because he cares for you" (1 Pet 5:5-7).

To Eat or Not to Eat: What Happens When You Fast
Fasting must be understood in a similar way. Giving up food as a

religious exercise produces neither piety points nor hunger-strike pressure which inclines God to answer prayer. (See Col 2:21-23; Lk 18:22; and Rom 14:17). Fasting helps many to think more clearly (because the head does not have to compete with the digestive organs for blood), and it can give anybody additional time in which to pray.

The issue involved in fasting is not food at all: "Food does not bring us near to God: we are no worse if we do not eat, and no better if we do" (1 Cor 8:8). The point is that the living God, who gives to us richly (1 Tim 6:17), somehow gets left out as we enjoy what he has given. We eat and drink and tell ourselves that our labor is good, but we forget that all things are from the hand of God. Abstinence gives us an opportunity to pull away a bit from the enjoyment of our blessings so as to concentrate on the One who is their source. Rightly understood, fasting should draw attention to God, not to the faster.[2] Hence Jesus instructs his disciples to "put oil on your head and wash your face, so that it will not be obvious to men that you are fasting, but only to your Father, who is unseen" (Mt 6:17-18).

Fasting is not commanded in the New Testament and some individual physiologies would not allow it even if it were. It should be undertaken with a specific prayer intention in mind (see Acts 13:2 and 14:27). If practiced regularly it can become a ritualistic source of self-service and self-gratification (Mt 6:16; Lk 18:12) which prevents fellowship and communion with God (Mt 6:1).

Paul suggests in 1 Corinthians 7:5-6 that "sexual fasting" may also help married couples. He sets three strict conditions: (1) that it be done by mutual agreement; (2) that it be done briefly, to be followed by normal intimacies; and (3) that the couple devote themselves to prayer. He does not say this because married sexuality is unspiritual or a hindrance to effective prayer. Married love is of divine origin, a "very flame of the LORD" (Song 8:6 NASB). Paul's advice stems from the fact that married love is interpersonally consuming. Two become one personally as well as physically. When a couple seeks to focus on God—when they desire intense concentration and communion with God—abstinence may help. "I say this as a concession, not as a command" (1 Cor 7:6).

Faith vs. Magic

Taken on their own, some of Jesus' statements about faith have been used to give the impression that faith gets results all by itself. In Matthew 9:22 he says, "Your faith has healed you." Here Jesus' words seem to suggest that faith had a direct action on the illness. But examining all three accounts of this incident (Mt 9:20-22; Mk 5:25-34; Lk 8:43-48) shows that the woman's approach to Jesus was based on the magical notion that if she touched Jesus' clothing she would be healed. She did so and was healed. But the source of the healing was not Jesus' garment; it was Jesus himself. He looked for the woman to correct her superstition. Jesus' complete response to her is given in Mark 5:34: "Daughter, your faith has saved you; go in peace, and be healed of your affliction." These words are a literal translation and may be taken as Mark's indication that the woman at that moment became a believer in Jesus' messiahship.[3]

Jesus next tells her, "Go in peace and be whole from your plague." This obviously refers to the permanent cessation of her hemorrhage (as distinct from her salvation) and indicates that Jesus, not his clothing, is responsible for the healing. Christ sought out the woman to make clear to her (and the crowd) the difference between belief in magic and personal faith in God's Son.

Faith is not a magical force which has direct action on the creation. People, from the biblical viewpoint, are not healed *by* faith, they are healed by God. Prayer, contrary to almost everything written about it, is not the most powerful force in the universe. God is. More things have *not* been wrought by prayer than this world thinks. More has been wrought *by God* in response to faith expressed through prayer than this world imagines. The point is not just a matter of semantics or an example of theological hair-splitting. It concerns a common and fundamentally mistaken conception about what prayer is and the role faith plays in it.

What happens when faith or prayer are thought to have inherent power is illustrated by Matthew 17:14-20. This is the case of the disciples' inability to exorcise the demon afflicting an epileptic boy. "Why couldn't we drive it out?" the disciples asked Jesus in private after his successful exorcism. He replied,

Because you have so little faith. I tell you the truth, if you have faith as small as a mustard seed, you can say to this mountain, "Move from here to there" and it will move. Nothing will be impossible for you.

The disciples asked, "Why can't *we* do it?" And Jesus' answer is, *God* must do it. They apparently began to feel that *they* had the power. Jesus' words mean: you are not trusting *in* God; you are trusting in yourselves. Mark tells us the Lord also said, "This kind can come out only by prayer" (Mk 9:29).[4] Prayer for Jesus is always an expression of human dependency on God and commitment to his power and will. The point Jesus makes in Mark 9:29 is, "*You* cannot do it; through prayer you must trust *God* to do it."

Since the smallest seed known to Jewish agriculture was selected to represent adequate faith, it is evident that the disciples' faith in God was nil. (That which is smaller than the smallest is nothing.) This conclusion seems certain in light of Jesus' initial characterization of the disciples as a faith*less* or *un*believing generation—something reported by all three Gospel writers (Mt 17:7; Mk 9:19; Lk 9:41). Luke says that after Jesus successfully exorcised the evil spirit and healed the boy, "they were all amazed at the greatness of God" (9:43). By not emphasizing Jesus' power, he ends the story leaving our attention focused on God.

Praying in the Face of Doubt

God should also be the focus in times of testing. There are times in the lives of even the most spiritual of God's children when faith is severely tested, when we begin to wonder whether God cares . . . or if he's even there at all. The last part of this chapter looks at those situations when having an attitude of dependence becomes extremely difficult.

Because the Bible is an honest book it contains prayers which are overt expressions of spiritual depression and complaint. Many Christians feel the way Habakkuk, Asaph, Job and David have felt. Despite persistence in prayer, circumstances can go from bad to worse:

How long, O LORD, must I call for help,
   but you do not listen?
Or cry out to you, "Violence!"
   but you do not save?
Why do you make me look at injustice?
   Why do you tolerate wrong? (Hab 1:2-3)

Surely in vain have I kept my heart pure;
   in vain I have washed my hands in innocence.
All day long I have been plagued;
   I have been punished every morning. (Ps 73:13-14)

Does it please you to oppress me,
   to spurn the work of your hands,
   while you smile on the schemes of the wicked?
Your hands shaped me and made me.
   Will you now turn and destroy me? (Job 10:3, 8)

My God, my God, why hast Thou forsaken me?
   Far from my deliverance are the words of my groaning.
O my God, I cry by day, but Thou dost not answer;
   And by night, but I have no rest. (Ps 22:1-2 NASB)

Such prayers seem to question God's benevolence and justice. Because of this some regard these complaints as sinful and blasphemous expressions of skepticism and unbelief. Yet such is not necessarily the case. Jesus himself once prayed some of these *same* words (Mt 27:46).

What do these prayers mean if they are not expressions of unbelief? First, despite their anger, frustration and even sarcasm, each line here is a statement that the petitioner believes God exists. These are not the mumblings of one resigned to fate, or the blind consolations of one singing, "Whatever will be, will be." These are prayers spoken to God. They are the sap which bleeds from a crushed and withering plant, sap which originates from old roots of faith which still cling to the soil of belief. Second, such prayers are declarations of honesty, recognitions of God's omniscience. These are the words of men who refuse to pretend, to mouth pious platitudes when inside they are hurting and churning. Third, these are prayers spoken by men who believe God's promises: to protect his own, to honor righteousness, to avenge wrong and display his justice. Fourth, these are prayers which assume God's omnipotence. They call for God to take action and display his strength. Last, these are prayers which ask, as all humans must due to their creatureliness, "Why? God, I don't understand." Because of this, these prayers are supplications seeking help and understanding uttered by men who see *no* source of deliverance and enlightenment other than God.

Such prayers may perhaps be classified as utterances of doubt, but they are not examples of skepticism and irreligion. They represent neither disobedience, lawlessness nor rebellion. They are petitions like that of the frustrated and desperate man who said to Jesus: "Lord have mercy!" and then, "If you can do anything, take pity on us and help us!" but finally, "I do believe, help me in my unbelief." In each case the author goes on to ask for restoration to fellowship, release from bitterness and frustration. David's prayer of complaint concerns God's discipline following his sin, "There is no soundness in my flesh because of Thine indignation; there is no health in my bones because of my sin" (Ps 38:3 NASB). He goes on to say, "Make haste to help me, O Lord, my salvation" (v. 22).

What is to be made of all this? First, it is better to pour out your heart and soul to God in honest expression of hurt, frustration and impatience than it is to repress these feelings and think they are hidden from God.[5] Second, when you are feeling this way, don't withdraw from worship. When Asaph came into the sanctuary of God things began to make more sense (Ps 73:16). Third, confess your sin and acknowledge your creatureliness. Frustration does not excuse unrighteousness and no man or woman is omniscient. Ask for restoration and renewed fellowship with God. Indulging in self-pity and persisting in isolation will only make matters worse. Fourth, spend time reading the Psalms and reflect honestly on your spiritual heritage. Others have been at such a point before and came through it. Things have not always been like this for you, nor are they going to remain this way forever. Jesus has also been where you are. He knew suffering, grief and experienced injustice, and now he prays for you (see Heb 4:14-16; 5:7-8). Finally, cling to the promise of Psalm 102:17. The Hebrew Masoretic heading for this prayer reads: "A prayer of the Afflicted, when he is faint, and pours out his complaint before the LORD" (NASB). To such a person, the Lord "will respond to the prayer of the destitute; he will not despise their plea."

I am convinced that even the forces of spiritual darkness are not sufficient to wrest our souls from the grace of God or permanently mar our usefulness to him. The care and nourishment of our faith rests ultimately, as Jesus told Peter, not in our ability to cope with our feelings, but in the faithfulness of God himself:

Simon, Simon, Satan has asked to sift you as wheat. But I have prayed for you, Simon, that your faith may not fail. And when you have turned back, strengthen your brothers. (Lk 22:31-32)

Holy Father, protect them by the power of your name. . . . My prayer is not that you take them out of the world but that you protect them from the evil one. They are not of the world, even as I am not of it. Sanctify them by the truth; your word is truth. . . . For them I sanctify myself, that they too may be truly sanctified. (Jn 17:11, 15-19)

I am convinced that neither death nor life, neither angels nor demons, neither the present nor the future, nor any powers, neither height nor depth, nor anything else in all creation, will be able to separate us from the love of God that is in Christ

Jesus our Lord. (Rom 8:37-39)
These texts suggest the ultimate basis for Christian faith and
prayer: the certainty that God has committed himself to us in
Christ, and the knowledge that his commitment is *always* and *in
everything* characterized by love.

Questions for Thought and Discussion

1. Do you think the author is right in claiming that it's hard for Christians used to
instant pudding, instant credit and instant replay to wait for anything? What does
your own experience suggest?
2. Does it make sense to say that Christians persist in prayer to express their *complete
dependency* on God? Are there other reasons for prayer persistence and importunity?
3. Is fasting spiritually helpful or harmful? What is its purpose?
4. Do you think that it is acceptable to pray like David, Habakkuk or Job in apparent
doubt and despair? Why? When have you felt this way?
5. What strategies have you employed to overcome doubt and despair?
6. Is there a difference between honest doubt and the doubt of skeptics? Do you
think God sees any difference?

Part 3
Jesus' Pattern
for Prayer

14
Christ: Our Example

During the early 1970s I worked with World Wide Pictures as an evangelist. I would accompany the films and explain the gospel message to those in attendance. This ministry proved to be both demanding and exciting. In our case, the entire family was involved. After helping us set up and watching film showings for several months, Doug—who was then about five—once regaled us with the following mimicry of the essentials of my ministry:

"All right, all you people. We've got a really *good* movie to show you tonight about Jesus. But *first*, we're going to take the offering. Give me *all* your loose money."

"Have I got it *all?*"

"O.K. Show the film."

No film presentation I ever did began quite like that! But I will never forget his monolog or the laughter which followed it. It is a vivid illustration of the ways we perceive and imitate people who are important to us.

We all look up to certain people, even after we grow tall enough to look them in the eye. Most of us have used people as models and consciously or unconsciously tried to imitate them. Historically the church has pointed to the Lord Jesus and exhorted the faithful to follow his example. In this chapter we look at the prayer experience of Jesus (as opposed to his teaching) as an example for Christians.

Can Jesus Be Our Example?

Christians are not united on the legitimacy of considering Jesus' prayer experience as an example for us. Objections tend to fall into two categories: (1) Jesus' experience is too *different* from ours to be applicable; and (2) it is too *personal* to be inquired into.

First, some say that since Jesus was God's Son and only took on the form of humanity, his experience with God was hardly normal enough to be our example. Jesus' prayer life was a special case, something too wonderful for us. He was the Shepherd, we are but sheep. He was divine and sinless, we are neither.

This way of thinking is motivated by a commendable desire to exalt the full divinity of Christ, something which has been minimized or even denied in much theological debate in our century. The Scriptures are unified in their proclamation of Jesus' divinity. Yet biblical authors are just as certain that Jesus was fully human. The appropriate response to denials of Jesus' divinity is not the negation of his humanity.

In the Incarnation, God's Son did not merely veil his divinity with skin—like Superman wears glasses and pretends to be Clark Kent. Rather, the eternal divine Word actually "became flesh"—*fully* human (Jn 1:14). When Philippians 2:7 talks about Jesus taking the *form* of a servant and having the *likeness* of a man, it means he became *by very nature* a man (NIV). The word *form* is the same word used to describe Jesus' divinity (Phil 2:5-7): his humanity was as real as his divinity. Our Lord did not merely appear to be human. He *was* human, and he called himself a man (Jn 8:40). "He had to be made like his brothers in every way . . . that he might make atonement for the sins of the people" (Heb 2:14-18).

Since Jesus in the fullness of his divinity took on our humanity, we need not fear that following the example of his humanity will demean or devalue his divine nature in any way. Except for the absence of a sin nature and, hence, personal sin, Jesus' humanity was no different than ours.

The second objection to seeing Jesus as our prayer example comes from another quarter. Some Christians, following scholars heavily steeped in existential philosophy, hold that prayer is so highly personal that it is an illegitimate invasion of privacy to examine how another may have prayed.

It's true that much of religious experience is personal or subjective. Some of us have become so zealous to defend the objective truth of God's written revelation that the faith can seem like a mere body of data: information to be examined, systematized and cataloged. Yet without the *objective* fact of Jesus' life and death, there could be no *personal* reconciliation. At its heart, Christianity is both objective and subjective.

The fact that prayer is personal does not negate the reality of objective standards which may govern its exercise. Precisely because prayer is communication between two subjects, without objective definition its words, no matter how personally moving their sound and fury to one party, may signify nothing to the other.

History shows that human nature has not changed since Jesus' day. So when I set out to talk with the immutable God, what may have been said before in conversation with him *is* relevant, no matter how long ago the interchange may have taken place. No, I cannot go back and pray Jesus' prayers. And we must pray now for ourselves. But we *can* learn from how Jesus prayed and seek to make his words our own.[1] The fact that he gave us the Lord's Prayer shows he felt the same way.

Jesus the Son

So how did Jesus pray? First, he prayed to God as Father. He used
the term *abba*, showing certainty that he was God's child. There is
never any sense that Jesus thought he had to get the Father's attention. Jesus had no doubt that the Father always loved him and
heard him. Even in his darkest hour Jesus' cry is not, "Father, how
could you let this happen to me if you really love me?" He says
instead, "Where are you?" (This prayer is a quotation of Psalm 22:1.
It goes on to say in verse 19, "O LORD, be not far off; O my
Strength, come quickly to help me.") That his Father cares and will
help, Jesus also never doubts. As a result he has confidence, which
means he always felt free to speak openly and honestly. Yet the
certainty of his Father's interest *never* results in the slightest hint of
arrogant boldness or disrespect for God's dignity. If God is *Abba*, he
is also the holy and righteous Father (Jn 17:11, 25), Lord of heaven
and earth (Lk 10:21).

So the first thing you must do to begin praying like Jesus is to
be certain about being God's child.[2] To those who have received
Christ in this way Paul says, "You are all sons of God through faith
in Christ Jesus. . . . Because you are sons, God sent the Spirit of his
Son into our hearts, the Spirit who calls out, '*Abba*, Father' " (Gal
3:26; 4:6).

Humble Dependence and Obedient Submission

The second thing we can learn from Jesus' example in prayer is how
to be obedient. Jesus said in Gethsemane: "Do you think I cannot
call on my Father, and he will at once put at my disposal more than
twelve legions of angels?" (Mt 26:53). Yet when his disciples tried
to protect him he declared, "Put your sword away! Shall I not drink
the cup the Father has given me?" (Jn 18:11). In the heat of crisis
Jesus was able to follow through in his lifelong pattern of submission to his Father's will. The climax of this came in prayer: "Yet not
my will, but yours be done" (Lk 22:42).

Our earliest picture of Jesus has him saying, "I must be about my
Father's business" (Lk 2:49 KJV). Later he would say, "My food is

to do the will of him who sent me" (Jn 4:34). And he summarized his life by saying, "I always do what pleases him" (Jn 8:29). Despite his own capabilities, Jesus' attitude was, "By myself I can do nothing" (Jn 5:19, 30). If ever there was a man with the right to declare his authority, it was Jesus. Yet his entire life was one of humble submission to God's will and word. He lived conscious of his dependency on the Father, and when he prayed, "he was heard because of his reverent submission" (Heb 5:7).

Developing an attitude of submission to God's will is not easy, particularly for people whom God has blessed. I was stopped short last year by a student who casually asked, "And how are you today, man of God?" Since I had worked hard at everything from cleaning floors on up and crossed an ocean (ten [sic] days at sea on a Greek freighter) to complete my education, I enjoyed the fantasy that I made myself into what I am today. But such a notion is pure baloney—sliced fairly thick. I had absolutely no control over my genetics, the selection of my parents and a thousand other things God has given me. Were it not for the unflagging encouragement of my wife I'd likely still be sitting in a very clean little room, alone on a stool, dissecting fruit flies. And I'd still be without Christ.

Man of God? Yes. All day, every day. There are *no* other kinds of men and women in the body of Christ. We receive only what is given to us from heaven. This is very easy to forget. But Jesus apparently remembered it, especially when he prayed. To pray like him we must stop breathing so much heady, reality-numbing, success-and-achievement gas and reflect more objectively on God.

Knowledge of God's Word

A third characteristic of Jesus' prayer life was that it was informed by God's Word. Repeatedly, in situation after situation, in public and in private, Jesus revealed an extensive knowledge of God based in Holy Scripture. We are not told how Jesus came by his knowledge of God's Word. In a normal first-century Jewish household, he would have been exposed to Scripture at home and at synagogue school. As an adult he attended the synagogue in Nazareth where the reading and explanation of the Scriptures were central parts of the service.

We may assume that Jesus spent much time reflecting on the sacred Jewish writings. He constantly appealed and alluded to, or directly quoted Holy Scripture. Probably Jesus gained a significant part of his understanding of God from the Old Testament. Scripture clearly shaped the way he called on God in prayer (compare Jn 11:41 and Ps 118:21; Lk 10:21 and Gen 14:22; Mk 15:34 and Ps 22:1).

God hears the prayers of believers who know no more Scripture than the verses printed on a tract. But since the Bible is our best source for understanding the mind of God, people who love him read his Word. Often they find themselves slipping into its wording when they pray.

To grow in prayer effectiveness you have to go to the Book—to read, to meditate on and to memorize it. Knowing God takes both time and effort. Do you expect God to hear you if you won't hear him?

Patterns in Jesus' Prayer Life

Jesus felt the need for prayer in a variety of mental states which reflect a wide gamut of normal human emotions. Luke says he prayed when "full of joy" (10:21), and John tells us there were other times when he expressed inner turmoil, "Now my heart is troubled, and what shall I say?" (12:27). He prayed with ease when in complete control of a situation (Mt 15:32-39) and in Gethsemane when needing angelic help to continue (Lk 22:43). He could be supremely confident of his commitment to do God's will (see Jn 17:19) and on the same evening struggle to the depths of his person: "My soul is overwhelmed with sorrow to the point of death" (Mk 14:34). He could find solace and strength in prayer alone with the Father (Lk 5:15; 6:12) and feel the need for others to "stay here and keep watch with me" (Mt 26:38). There were times when he expressed certainty that the Father always heard him (Jn 11:42) and another time when he anguished in the emotional pain of loneliness (Mk 15:34).

Jesus' experiences confirm that any time and any place are appropriate for prayer. They also establish that one may go to the Father in any mental and emotional condition. There is no need to pretend we're up when we're down. And the Father wants to share our joys as much as he wants to be our support in times of great need.

Jesus' prayer experience included participating in worship. He regularly attended the local synagogue and seems to have gone frequently to the national religious assemblies, or feasts, in Jerusalem (Lk 22:15; Jn 2:23; 7:14; 12:12). Prayer was a feature in all Jewish religious observances and festivals. Jesus probably kept the regular (Jewish) schedule of offering prayers three times a day (Dan 6:10; Mt 6:5). We know he was offended by the Temple officials' turning of the place of public prayer into an institution of extortion (Mk 11:17). And we may take it that Jesus often prayed among other worshipers.

Corporate Jewish worship in Jesus' day involved set prayers based on a form of liturgy which borrowed heavily from the Old Testament. If our Savior participated in such services, then Christians today may also affirm the legitimacy and efficacy of liturgical prayer. Prayer books are *not* invitations to mindless mumbling. The use of liturgical prayer gives the congregation a pattern which allows them to know what will be said next. This avoids a difficulty faced by those in nonliturgical services: mentally one must be both critical (analyzing what's being said so as to know whether you too can affirm it) and spiritual (seeking communion with God) at the same time. But liturgical or extemporaneous, the need for active listening and thinking about the words being prayed is vital: without it we are effectively not there.

Yet private prayer is also essential to vital worship. Jesus clearly did not regard public services as "enough" for the week, nor did he use his devotional life as an excuse for not participating with others. Jesus' life showed a balance between public and private prayer.

Jesus also customarily offered grace, a benediction or thanksgiving to God, before eating (Mk 8:6; Jn 11:6; compare Lk 22:17, 19).

This may have been such a distinctive practice with Jesus that he was known for doing so in a special way. In Luke 24:30-31 Christ is recognized following his resurrection only after he prayed (offered grace) and broke the bread.

Mothers apparently thought Jesus such a man of prayer that little children were brought to Jesus for him to place his hands on them and pray for them (Mt 19:13). He did not consider himself so busy with weightier (adult) matters that children did not count. Jesus' prayers encompassed an extremely wide spectrum: from the guilelessness of children to the guilt of his executioners (Lk 23:34).

Like Jesus' prayers, his prayer postures were varied. References in the Gospels probably are not all-inclusive.[3] The Gospel writers tell us he prayed standing, while looking up to heaven (Jn 11:41; 17:1; compare Lk 18:11, 13; 1 Tim 2:8); kneeling (Lk 22:41); falling to the ground (Mk 14:35); and prostrate with his face to the ground (Mt 26:39). These descriptions reflect different moods and circumstances but all are either expressions of expectancy (looking up) or humble dependency and supplication (kneeling and prostration).

Jesus was heard no matter what position he used. The same is true for us. We cannot let our freedom in this offend the traditions or cultures of others. But when you are alone with God, be yourself. Let the content, circumstances, emotions and time of the prayer determine your position. Remember his holiness and focus on God, not on what you are wearing, doing, or how you might look to someone else. Don't let your own superstitions (or someone else's insecurity) obligate you to pray on your knees in a dark closet if you want to walk with God on a mountain in the sunrise. The veil into the Temple was ripped wide open by God himself. Religious ritual and routine expired with Jesus on the cross. Don't forget it when you pray.

Given Jesus' sinlessness, it comes as no surprise that Jesus never offered a prayer of confession or asked for forgiveness and cleansing. (The Lord's Prayer is introduced with, "When you pray, *you* say . . .") But analysis shows that Jesus offered prayer in all the other biblical categories: praise (Lk 10:21); blessing (Lk 24:50); thanksgiving (Jn 6:11; 11:41); petition (Lk 22:42; Jn 17:1-5); and intercession (Mk 10:16; Lk 22:32; 23:34; Jn 17:6-26).

The type of prayer mentioned most frequently in the Gospels is Jesus' thanksgiving and blessing of God. Yet the writers have actually given the most space (number of verses) to his intercessory prayers on behalf of others. Jesus' gratitude for God's goodness led him to seek blessing for others. His emphasis on thanksgiving and intercession seems nothing more than the practical outworking in prayer of the Savior's understanding of true religion: to love God totally, without reservation, and to love others even more than we do our own life. This does not make other types of prayer less important; it just shows us where his heart was . . . and is. How much time do you give to thanksgiving and intercession when you pray?

Prayer: A Personal Priority

Prayer was vital in Jesus' ministry. He saw it as essential to accomplishing God's will (compare Mt 6:10; Mk 14:36; Jn 17). Jesus prayed a long time before selecting his disciples (compare Lk 4:42— 5:11; 6:12-13). He prayed before his miracles (see Jn 6:11; 11:41), and he said of the exorcism of certain demons, "this kind can come out only by prayer" (Mk 9:29). He spontaneously praised God for his disciples' success (Mt 11:25) and prayed for them in times of failure and coming trouble (Lk 22:32; Jn 17:6-19). He knew times of great intensity in prayer (Lk 22:44), and in Gethsemane he persisted while repeating the same prayer three times (Mt 26:44). Before an important decision he once prayed all night (Lk 6:12). Obviously, Jesus' prayer communion with God was sometimes personally consuming. The fact that he was transfigured and assumed divine glory while he was praying (Lk 9:28-29) indicates something like this.

In contrast to Jesus, most of us are too busy coping with existence to see prayer as vital or essential. But life *could* be more simple. An older car, a less trendy wardrobe, reupholstered rather than replaced furniture, a littleless meat on the table—changes like this could reduce the need for so much income and perhaps provide more time for prayer. Part of the reason Jesus had time and energy to pray the way he did was the simplicity of his life. He owned next to nothing and invested his life in people, ideas, conversations and relationships. He viewed success quite differently than we usually do. And he viewed *whatever* he did as God's work. These are thoughts worth pondering . . . even if they are also threatening. Who are you really in love with? Is it God? Your spouse? Your children? Friends? Success? Your image? Where is your treasure? There your heart is also. Prayer is basically a matter of priorities, isn't it?

Questions for Thought and Discussion

1. How do you want to be like Jesus? What seems most attractive about him to you?
2. What does it mean to pray in boldness and confidence?
3. How would you feel if someone called you a man or woman of God? Why is that title disconcerting?
4. Do you prefer liturgical or extemporaneous prayers? Why are certain types of prayer more meaningful to you?
5. What practical suggestions regarding methods for prayer (time of day, place, position, content and so on) have most helped you? Share these with others.

15
Concluding:
What's in
Jesus' Name?

From the time I was born people have called me "Bing." As a youngster I thought nothing of it. But it has presented some difficulties. I get tired sometimes of being asked if I can sing, "I'm Dreeeaamming of a Whiiiitte Christ-mas." In high school there was an immortal song with the lyrics, "ting, tang, wala-wala, BING, bang." And after college, the immense masculine satisfaction I felt for winning Jo-Ann's heart was eroded in a reception line following our wedding when an old family friend said, "So you're the girl who married little Bingie!" The editor of a scholarly journal has addressed me as "Der Bingle," and one Sunday in a church in Cambridge, England—where one *does* want to be dignified—it was announced that "Bingley" would give the morning message. I don't know about you, but I notice what people do with my name. And

chances are our Lord has at least as much interest in what people
do with his.

In Jesus' Name
I was told as a young Christian that the phrase *in Jesus' name* was
essential to God's hearing my prayer. Without it prayers would not
get through. I remember wondering subsequently if a prayer I
heard offered with a naked *Amen* at the end would really work.
Later I noticed that some saints tended to pray with much emphasis
on *in Jesus' name*, often drawing the words out and expressing real
emotion. Others seemed just to tack them on at the end, almost as
an afterthought. More recently I have met persons who hold that
invoking Jesus' name has direct power of its own. And once I was
confronted by a very zealous believer who explained that praying
in Jesus' name would actually *force* the Father to give me *whatever* I
asked.

There are other ideas, but most boil down to one of these three:
(1) the phrase is quasimagical, a kind of sanctified "Open Sesame";
(2) it functions a bit like the secret number issued by banks to
operate cash machines—*in Jesus' name* authenticates an account
holder so a transaction can be processed; or (3) the words activate
a kind of spiritual leverage or clout to which God responds because
of the authority of the Savior's name.

All three notions are shown to be errors by Luke's somewhat hu-
morous account of a botched exorcism in which invoking Jesus'
name had absolutely no effect whatsoever (Acts 19:8-10). But if
these common notions are false, what purpose do these words
serve?

The Biblical Evidence
Jesus' invitation to pray "in my name" is found only in his last
discourse, in John 14—16. And it may surprise some to learn that
the rest of the New Testament contains only one explicit reference
to prayer in this manner: "Sing and make music in your heart to
the Lord, always giving thanks to God the Father for everything,

in the name of our Lord Jesus Christ" (Eph 5:19-20).

Given the fact that the New Testament contains many prayers, the paucity of this phrase is significant.[1] The early church probably did not regard Jesus' words as a rubric or formula for prayer and probably invested them with other significance.[2]

In John 14—16, *in my name* is used in connection with prayer in three different ways. First, there are references to *asking the Father* in Jesus' name:

Until now you have not asked for anything in my name. Ask . . . and your joy will be complete. . . . In that day you will ask in my name. I am not saying that I will ask the Father on your behalf. No, the Father himself loves you because you have loved me and have believed that I came from God. (16:24, 26)

Second, one text refers to *asking Jesus himself* in Jesus' name:[3] "And I will do whatever you ask in my name, so that the Son may bring glory to the Father. You may ask me for anything in my name, and I will do it" (14:13-14). Third, there's a statement that *the Father gives* answers to prayer "in Jesus' name": "Truly, truly, I say to you, if you shall ask the Father for anything, He will give it to you in My name" (16:23 NASB).[4]

The first category here is well known and is behind the popular prayer theology which suggests that prayer is rightly offered when it is made *to* the Father *through* the Son. The idea that Jesus is our advocate is well grounded elsewhere, as we shall see. But our second group of verses clearly envisions prayer being offered directly *to* Jesus himself—and that *he* does the answering. Taken together the three groups of verses show that *in my name* somehow conditions prayer offered to both the Father and the Lord Jesus. It also apparently applies in some way to the answer as well. Clearly the phrase conveyed more to the Savior than it seems to when we tack it on at the end of a petition. Consideration of other evidence in John will help us understand its meaning.

Abiding and Obeying

When we read the six verses quoted above we notice that Jesus gives our asking no limits:

14:13—*whatever* you ask in my name
14:14—ask me *anything* in my name
16:23—ask the Father for *anything* . . . he will give . . . in my name
16:24—not asked for *anything* in my name

Jesus' teaching about this kind of prayer always promises a divine response. In addition, Jesus' statements about these prayers have three other elements: (1) a verb for petition; (2) the statement of scope ("anything"); and (3) the *in my name* phrase.

By examining the whole of Jesus' last discourse in John 14—16, we may find keys to the meaning of *in my name* as Christ used it. Can we find similar sentences where Jesus used the first two elements mentioned above (a verb for petition and a statement of scope) but replaced the *in my name* phrase with something else?

	Verb for Petition	Statement of Scope	Name Phrase
We have:	"Ask"	"anything"	"in my name"
We want:	"Ask"	"anything"	?

Jesus made such a statement (though the word order is different) in John 15:7: "If you abide in Me, and My words abide in you, ask whatever you wish, and it shall be done for you" (NASB). Diagrammed it looks like this:

Verb for Petition	Statement of Scope	Name Phrase Equivalent
ask	whatever you wish	if you abide in Me and My words abide in you

This suggests the provisional conclusion that Jesus used *in my name* to mean about the same thing as "abiding" in Christ and having his words "abide" in us. But what does it mean to abide in Christ?[5] The Greek word *(meno)* which some Bible translations render "abide" can be translated other ways, including "remain," "dwell" and "continue." But what we need is a *definition* for *abiding in Christ.* John 15:10 looks promising: "If you keep My commandments, you will abide in My love" (NASB). But *abide in my love* is not quite the same thing as *abide in me.* But in his first letter the apostle John has given us a crystal-clear definition of *abide in me:* "The one who keeps His commandments abides in Him" (3:24 NASB). The verse makes it plain that practically speaking abiding in Christ boils down to obeying his teaching. Though scholars tend to define abiding as a kind of mystical union between the Savior and believers, it is not so much mystical as it is volitional.

If we substitute this definition of *abiding* in John 15:7, we end up with:

Verb of Petition	Statement of Scope	Name Phrase Equivalent
ask	whatever you wish	if you keep my commandments and my words abide in you

This brings us to the conclusion that asking *in Jesus' name* relates somehow to the petitioner's *obedience* to Jesus' commandments. Such obedience is not coerced, but is actively desired by all in whom Jesus lives through his Spirit. Keeping Jesus' commandments and having his words abide in us mean the same thing. "There is *no* practical difference between Jesus' personal indwelling in his disciples and his words remaining in them," says F. F. Bruce.[6] John Stott also makes the connection: "It is *only* when Christ's words abide in us that our prayers will be answered. Then we can ask what we will and it shall be done, because we shall will only what he wills."[7]

This is what I have called the prayer-obedience cycle. When

Christ's word becomes internalized through training facilitated by obedience, we begin to think God's thoughts, which helps us pray according to his will: Obedience helps us will and pray what Christ wills.

That this connection of prayer and obedience is appropriate is confirmed by John 15:16: "You did not choose me, but I chose you to go and bear fruit—fruit that will last. Then the Father will give you whatever you ask in my name." This verse makes fruit-bearing an antecedent to the Father's answering our prayers.[8] Fruit-bearing has been understood as a reference to personal moral qualities (such as those listed in Gal 5:22), good works (referred to in Col 1:10) or new converts (mentioned in Jn 4:36). But such fruit-bearing *always* comes through obedience to Jesus' teaching and recognition of our dependency on him. Notice that after John 15:7, Jesus went on to focus on obedience as a demonstration that we are his disciples, his friends.

Obedience

What does it mean then to pray in Jesus' name? First, the *objective* of prayer offered in Jesus' name is the glorification of God. This is unmistakable in 14:13, "I will do whatever you ask in my name, so that the Son may bring glory to the Father." The central concern of one who prays in this way is God himself, not the granting of petitions. The structure of the Lord's Prayer reflects this, as it begins with, "Hallowed be *thy* name, *thy* kingdom come . . ." This kind of preoccupation with God characterized our Savior. To pray in his name, we must be similarly engrossed with God's glory.

Second, prayer offered in Jesus' name is made *only* on the merits or basis of Jesus' work, not on our own.[9] The death and resurrection of Jesus are the *sole* ground on which rests Christian communication with God: "In him and through faith in him we may approach God with freedom and confidence" (Eph 3:12). Christ's words *in my name* contain implicitly everything which is developed later in the New Testament. He is the one and only true, living way to God.

Third, those who pray in Jesus' name claim to represent him, and hence should be his true disciples. Salespeople sign orders in the name of companies, and lawyers take legal actions in the name of their clients. Jesus, as the Revealer and Son of God, said, "I have come in my Father's name" (Jn 5:43). He claimed he did his supernatural works on God's behalf. In a similar way, we who pray in Jesus' name should be Christ's genuine disciples and engaged in his work. When this is not true, we have no legitimate claim to represent him. Jesus made the identification of his followers very simple: "If you hold to my teaching, you are really my disciples" (Jn 8:31); "If you love me, you will obey what I command" (Jn 14:15).

Finally, those who come to God in Jesus' name seek to pray as Jesus himself would have prayed in the same situation. I base this observation on the way the Bible uses the term *name*. In Scripture the name of a person stands for what that individual is and does. The name is so closely identified with the person that, in many cases, the name effectively equals the person. The psalmist says, "May the *name* of the God of Jacob protect you" (20:1); "I will call on the *name* of the Lord" (116:13). Here the word *name* stands for God himself.[10]

This is also true in the New Testament. When John speaks of "those who believed *in his name*" (1:12; compare 2:23), he refers to faith in Jesus himself.[11] Those who pray in Jesus' name are so identifying themselves and their petitions with our Lord that they in effect claim to pray what the Savior himself would.

Speaking about the meaning of the expression *pray in my name*, Bishop Westcott once said, "The meaning of the phrase is 'as being one with me even as I am revealed to you.' . . . There is exact conformity between the disciples' prayer and Christ's will."[12] Likewise, Samuel Chadwick taught,

> To pray in the Name of Christ . . . is to pray as one who is at one with Christ, whose mind is the mind of Christ, whose desires are the desires of Christ, and whose purpose is one with that of Christ.[13]

Thus those who pray in Jesus' name must always ask themselves,

What would Christ pray for in this situation? Prayer from the mind of Christ is always according to God's will, and hence is always heard—as Jesus himself said in John 11:41. This would explain why *in my name* prayers are all unconditional: "you will receive *anything* you ask." Again, we are talking about how the prayer-obedience cycle works.

In summary I believe that prayer in Jesus' name includes four components:[14]

☐ It seeks the glory of God.

☐ Its foundation is the death, resurrection and intercession of Jesus.

☐ It is offered by Jesus' obedient disciples.

☐ It asks what Jesus himself would pray for.

I have summarized what we know about how our Lord prayed in the previous chapter. But the shortest and perhaps the best answer is simply: Jesus *prayed according to the will of God.* And that, ultimately, is what it means for you and I to pray in Jesus' name—to pray according to the will of God. You will find that the phrase *according to God's will* can be substituted in each of the prayer verses quoted earlier, and it makes sense of the fact that *in my name* conditions both our asking and the Father's giving:

Prayer: Anything you ask *according to God's will,* you will receive.

Answer: God will give *in accordance with his will* anything you ask.

Put differently, when we pray in Jesus' name we receive whatever we ask because our will and God's will are the same. We pray according to God's will when we respond to the Creator as he really is, in light of his nature and attributes, his character, his personality. And we pray in the will of God when we respond in faith as his child to his Fatherly love and concern. Through obedience—through the prayer-obedience cycle—the Spirit helps us come to understand our Creator and what it means to be his child. Prayer in Jesus' name is offered by those who seek God's will and glory through obedience to the word of his Son. *All* distinctively Christian prayer is offered in Jesus' name. This helps to explain a tension we all feel about the apparently limitless prayer promises in the first three Gospels. In his teaching recorded in Matthew, Mark and Luke, the Savior *assumes* what John tells us he made explicit in his last discourse: that his true disciples would not desire to ask *anything* which is outside the will of their heavenly Father.

In the End

You will no doubt recognize that we have come back to where we started all those pages ago, to the definition of prayer given in the first chapter:

Prayer is a means God uses to give us what he wants.

And that is the point of this book. Who does God hear? He hears those who pray and live to glorify him.

Delight yourself in the Lord and he will give you the desires of your heart.

Questions for Thought and Discussion

1. How do Christians you know understand the use of *in Jesus' name* for prayer?
2. John 14:13-14 suggests Jesus expected Christians to pray to him as well as the Father. Why are some Christians troubled by this idea?
3. Are you convinced that prayer and obedience are related? How?
4. In what way is praying in Jesus' name the same as praying according to God's will?
5. If you think of prayer in God's name as prayer according to God's will, does it explain why some recent prayers of yours were not answered? Does it help to know that? Why or why not?

Appendix:
Scriptures
on Prayer

One of the often neglected (yet most fruitful) areas for Bible study is the topic of prayer. But I have discovered that many Christians are quite interested in such an investigation. They are just not certain where to look. The most comprehensive listing of biblical prayer material generally available is contained in Herbert Lockyer's *All the Prayers of the Bible*.[1] The list which follows is not as complete, but it may be a good place to start on a study of prayer.

As you work with this material remember that one of the *essentials* in good biblical interpretation is to avoid analysis of isolated verses. *Always* read the material which comes both before and after your text and you will understand more clearly what the author is saying.

Start with the prayers of Jesus in John or Mark, and then widen the scope of your study gradually. Read the prayers of Paul in Colossians and Ephesians and compare the different approaches taken by the Savior and his apostle. I recommend you get into the prayer teaching texts last; the didactic material is more complicated. If you get stuck on a verse, get some help from a Bible-believing commentator. The *New Bible Commentary: Revised* (Eerdmans) is usually helpful, but as a one-volume work it sometimes does not cover the verse you want. When this happens a commentary from a multivolume set will usually help. Your pastor or an elder can probably give you advice (and maybe loan you the book). Generally helpful works still in print if you want to buy such books are the Tyndale Biblical Commentaries (Old Testament: InterVarsity Press; New Testament: Eerdmans), the New International Commentaries (Eerdmans), the Expositor's Bible Commentaries (Zondervan) and the New Testament Commentary (Baker).

When you use a commentary continue to think for yourself, take notes and rephrase things in your own words. Talk over questionable interpretations with friends, your pastor or an elder. If the whole business of Bible study is new to you, it would be worth your time to get and work through Walter Henrichsen's *A Layman's Guide to Interpreting the Bible* (Zondervan & NavPress) and James W. Sire's *Scripture Twisting* (InterVarsity Press). Both books are understandable, written for the nonspecialist and full of good helps and hints. Walt Henrichsen will show you how to do it and Jim Sire will show you what happens when you don't do it right.

Whether you do your study by yourself or with helps, always press on beyond the data to delve into your own life. Ask, What does this mean to me? to the way I live? to the way I pray? What have I learned about God here? How will that change the way I talk to him and others? What can I share of this with others? Let the text get inside: hear the Word of the living God. Don't just catalog it as the abstractions of theology and ancient history. No matter how old you are, as you study the material on this list try to have the expectant attitude of young Samuel. Before you begin, pray as he did: "Speak, LORD, for your servant is listening" (1 Sam 3:9).

List of Scripture passages relevant to the study of prayer
Important prayers of the Old Testament:

Genesis 18:22-33	Abraham prays for Sodom	Exodus 15:1-18	Moses praises God
Genesis 24:12-14	Prayer for guidance	Exodus 32:7-14 32:30-34 }	Moses prays for a sinful people
Genesis 27:27-29	Isaac prays for Jacob	Exodus 33:11-23	Moses asks to see God
Genesis 28:10-22	Jacob makes vows to God	Exodus 34:29-35	Moses reflects the glory of God
Genesis 32:9-12	Jacob pleads with God	Leviticus 16:1-34	Forgiveness through sacrifice
Genesis 48:15-16 49:1-29 }	Prophetic prayer by Jacob	Numbers 14:1-45	Moses prays for a faithless people
Exodus 3:1—4:17	Moses talks with God	Deuteronomy 9:7-29	Moses' intercession remembered

Deuteronomy 32:1-43	Moses praises God's greatness	1 Kings 18:41-46	Elijah prophesies, then prays for rain
Deuteronomy 33:1-29	Moses blesses the people before he dies	1 Kings 19:1-18	God's quiet voice in depression
Joshua 7:6-15	Prayer of the humiliated	2 Kings 19:1-37	Hezekiah prays for God's honor
Joshua 10:12-14	Prayer for a miracle is heard	2 Kings 20:1-11	Hezekiah prays for his life
Judges 5:2-31	Deborah praises the Lord	1 Chronicles 16:7-36	David gives glory to God's name
Judges 6:11-40	Gideon prays for certainty in guidance	1 Chronicles 17:16-27	David's thanks for an eternal dynasty
Judges 19:1— 21:25	Leaderless and prayerless: Disaster	1 Chronicles 29:10-20	David prays for his son, Solomon
Ruth 2:12, 20 3:10; 4:14 }	Boaz answers his own prayer	1 Chronicles 36:15-21	God's pity, the people's mockery: Jerusalem utterly destroyed!
1 Samuel 1:9-17	Hannah weeps before the Lord	Ezra 9:1-15	Ezra confesses for the nation
1 Samuel 2:1-10	Hannah exalts the Rock, the Lord	Nehemiah 1:4-10	Nehemiah asks God to remember
1 Samuel 7:2-14	Samuel brings the people back to God	Nehemiah 4:9	We prayed and posted a guard
1 Samuel 15:22-23	Worship without obedience rejected	Nehemiah 9:1-37	The people repent of their sins
1 Samuel 20:12-23	The prayer of true friends	Job 10:2-22	The prayer of a desperate man
2 Samuel 7:18-29	David's thanks for an eternal dynasty	Job 12:1—13:22	The pleading of a soul in anguish
2 Samuel 22:2-51	David's hymn of praise to the Most High	Job 42:2-6	Job sees, understands and repents
2 Samuel 24:10-25	David repents and the Lord relents		
1 Kings 3:4-15	Solomon prays for wisdom		
1 Kings 8:22-61	Solomon dedicates the Temple		
1 Kings 9:2-9	God replies to Solomon at Gibeon		
1 Kings 18:16-39	Elijah prays; God answers by fire		

The Psalms are nearly all prayers of one type or another. You should study the whole book systematically. In a sense it is the very soul of Scripture: a dialog with God on every page. Some of the highlights of the Psalter are:

Psalm 4	Evening prayer
Psalm 5	Morning prayer
Psalm 23	The shepherd psalm

Psalms 24; 67; 92; } Praise and wor-
95-98; 100; 113; } ship
145; 148; 150 }

Psalm 25   Guidance
Psalms 37; 62   Trust
Psalms 40; 116   Deliverance
Psalms 27; 42; 63; Longing for God
84
Psalms 51; 130   Forgiveness
Psalms 65; 111; 136 Thanksgiving
Psalms 66; 69; 86; } Help in trouble
88; 102; 140; 143 }
Psalms 89; 103; }   God's constant
107; 146 }   love and care
Psalms 8; 29; 93;   God's majesty and
104   glory
Psalm 139   God's knowledge
                    and presence
Psalms 19; 119   God's Word
Psalms 46; 91; 125 God's protection
This listing of Psalms has been taken from Eerd-
man's Handbook to the Bible.

Isaiah 6:1-13   Isaiah sees the
                    Lord!
Isaiah 25:1-8   A hymn of praise
                    to the Lord Al-
                    mighty
Isaiah 33:2-24   Prayer for help
                    and forgiveness
Isaiah 37:14-20   Hezekiah prays
                    for deliverance
Isaiah 38:1-21   Prayer for heal-
                    ing; praise for
                    answer
Isaiah 63:7—64:12   O Lord, you are
                    our Father
Jeremiah 10:23—   Jeremiah prays
11:17   and God replies
                    with woe
Jeremiah 14:10-17   Jeremiah forbid-
                    den to pray for Is-
                    rael
Jeremiah 20:7-18   Jeremiah prays in
                    depression
Jeremiah 32:17-44   Jeremiah asks the

Lamentations   Lord to deliver
1:1—4:22   and God replies
                    Jeremiah's prayer
                    of lament for Is-
                    rael
Lamentations 5:1-   Jeremiah's prayer
22   for God to restore
                    his people
Ezekiel 4:12-16   The prophet
                    prays in revulsion
Ezekiel 9:1-11   Are You going to
                    destroy them all?
Ezekiel 11:13-21   A plea with God's
                    sovereign reply
Daniel 2:17-23   A prayer for help
                    answered
Daniel 4:34-37   The rejoicing of a
                    king restored
Daniel 6:1-28   Faithfulness in
                    prayer rewarded
Daniel 9:3-19   Daniel confesses
                    Israel's sins
Amos 7:1-9   Spared twice
                    through prayer
Jonah 2:1-10   Jonah prays when
                    he's "down in the
                    mouth"
Jonah 3:1-10   The Ninevites re-
                    pent before God
Jonah 4:1-10   The prophet
                    pouts in prayer
Habakkuk 1:2-4,   Habakkuk com-
12-17   plains to God
Habakkuk 3:1-19   Habakkuk wor-
                    ships and rejoices
Zechariah 1:2-6   God's people repent
Zechariah 7:1-14   The people ask
                    God about fasting
Malachi 1:2, 6-7; } God is mocked
2:17; 3:7-8; 3:13 } through prayer

Prayer in the New Testament
The Prayers of Jesus
Matthew 11:25- } A prayer of
26 } thanksgiving

Luke 10:21
John 11:41-42 — Prayer at Lazarus's grave
John 12:27-28 — A prayer when troubled
John 17:1-26 — The real "Lord's Prayer"
Matthew 26:36-46 }
Mark 14:32-42 } The struggle in the garden
Luke 22:39-46 }
Luke 23:34 — Father, forgive them . . .
Matthew 27:46 }
Mark 15:34 } Why have You forsaken me?
Luke 23:46 — Father, receive my spirit

References to prayer in Jesus' life

Luke 3:21 — Prayer at Jesus' baptism
Mark 1:35 }
Luke 5:16 } Prayer in the desert
Luke 6:12-13 — Prayer before selecting his disciples
Matthew 14:19 }
Mark 6:41 }
Luke 9:16 } Prayer before feeding 5,000
John 6:11 }
Matthew 14:23 }
Mark 6:46 } Prayer alone on a mountain
Mark 7:34 — Prayer for a deaf mute
Matthew 15:36 }
Mark 8:6 } Prayer before feeding 4,000
Luke 9:18 — Jesus prays alone
Luke 9:28-29 — Jesus transfigured while praying
Matthew 19:13-14 }
Mark 10:13-16 } Jesus prays for the children
Matthew 26:26-27 }
Mark 14:22-23 } God blessed at the Lord's Supper
Luke 22:17-19 }

Luke 22:31-32 — Jesus prays for Peter
Hebrews 5:7-8 — Agony in Gethsemane recalled
Matthew 26:53 — Potential prayer for legions of angels
Luke 24:30-31 — God blessed for food in Emmaus
Luke 24:50-51 — Jesus ascends while blessing his men

Petitions addressed to Jesus

John 4:47-49 — A nobleman asks help for his son
Matthew 8:2 }
Mark 1:40 } A leper begs for healing
Luke 5:12 }
Matthew 8:6 }
Luke 7:6-7 } A centurion seeks help for a servant
Matthew 8:25 }
Mark 4:38 } Lord, save us from the storm
Luke 8:24 }
Matthew 8:29 }
Mark 5:7 } A demoniac's plea
Luke 8:28 }
Matthew 9:18 }
Mark 5:22-23 } Jairus seeks help for his little girl
Luke 8:41-42 }
Matthew 9:27-28 — The blind beg to be healed
Matthew 14:30 — Peter asks for safety in the storm
Matthew 15:21-28 }
Mark 7:24-30 } The persistant woman
Matthew 17:14-15 }
Mark 9:17-18 } A father seeks healing for his boy
Luke 9:38-40 }
Luke 17:12-13 — Ten lepers ask to be cleansed
Matthew 20:30-33 }
The blind men of Jericho seek sight

Mark 10:47-51
Luke 18:38-41
Luke 23:42   The prayer of the
                     thief on the cross

The prayer teaching of Jesus

Matthew	Mark	Luke	John
5:44	7:6-7	5:33	4:23-24
6:5-15	11:17	6:28	14:12-14
7:7-11	11:23-24	6:46	15:7
9:38	12:40	10:2	15:16
15:8-9	13:18	11:1-13	16:23-27
18:19-20	13:33	17:18	
21:13		18:1-14	
21:21-22		19:46	
24:20		20:47	
		21:36	

Other references to prayer in the Gospels

Luke 1:10	Luke 1:46-55	Luke 2:29-32	Luke 24:52-53
Luke 1:13	Luke 1:64, 67-79	Luke 2:37-38	John 9:31

References to prayer in the Book of Acts

1:13-14	8:22-24	13:2-3	20:36
1:24-25	9:5-11	14:23	21:4
2:42	9:13-14	15:28	22:7-11
3:1	9:40	15:40	22:17-21
3:8	10:1-8	16:6-9	23:11
4:8-12	10:9-16	16:13, 16	26:13-15
4:24-31	10:30	16:25	27:21-25
6:4, 6	11:4-11	18:9-10	27:35
7:59-60	11:18	19:6	28:8
8:14-17	12:5-12	20:32	28:15

References to prayer in the New Testament Letters
Key: * = a prayer; + = benediction or doxology

Romans	+ 11:33-36	1 Corinthians	+ 16:23
* 1:7-9	12:12	* 1:3-7	
1:21	14:6	1:14	2 Corinthians
8:15	+ 15:5-6	2:13	* 1:2-4
8:26-27	+ 15:13	7:5	1:11
8:34	15:30-33	11:4-5	2:14
9:1-4	16:20	11:24	4:15
10:1-2	+ 16:25-27	14:14-17	8:16
10:9-13		14:18	9:12

9:14	4:2-3	4:14	5:4
12:6-10	4:12	+ 4:20, 23	5:13-18
13:7	4:18		
+ 13:14		*Titus*	*1 Peter*
	1 Thessalonians	* 1:4	* 1:2-3
Galatians	* 1:2-3	+ 3:15	1:17
* 1:3-5	3:9-13		2:9
2:2	5:17-18	*Philemon*	3:7
4:6	5:25	* 3-4	3:9
+ 6:18	+ 5:23, 28	22	3:12
		+ 25	4:7
Ephesians	*2 Thessalonians*		5:5-6
+ 1:2-3	1:2-4	*Hebrews*	5:10-11
1:16-17	1:11-13	2:12	+ 5:14
* 3:14-19	2:16-17	2:16-18	
+ 3:20-21	3:1-2	4:13-16	*2 Peter*
5:17-20	3:5	5:7	* 1:2
6:18-20	+ 3:16	7:24-25	+ 3:18
+ 6:23-24	+ 3:18	9:12	
		* 10:5-7	*1 John*
Philippians	*1 Timothy*	10:10	1:9
* 1:2-5	* 1:2	12:14	2:1-2
1:9	1:12-13	12:28-29	3:22
1:19	1:17	13:15	5:14-16
2:11	2:1-2	13:18	
2:13	2:8	+ 13:20-21	*2 John*
2:27	4:3-5	+ 13:35	* 3
3:15	5:5		
4:6-7	+ 6:21	*James*	*3 John*
4:11		1:5-7	* 2
+ 4:20, 23	*2 Timothy*	1:17	
	* 1:2-4	3:9	*Jude*
Colossians	1:16	4:2-6	* 2
* 1:2-3	1:18	4:13-15	+ 24-25
1:9			

Prayer and Worship in the Book of Revelation

1:4-6	5:13	8:3-4	19:1-3
4:6-8	6:9-11	11:16-19	19:4-8
4:10-11	6:16	15:3-4	22:9
5:8-10	7:9-12	16:5-7	22:20-21

Notes

Chapter 1: Who Does God Hear?

[1]Friedrich Heiler, *Das Gebet: Eine religionsgeschichtliche und religionspsychologische Untersuchung*, 5th ed. (München and Basel: E. Reinhardt, 1969), p. 1.

[2]"Can Modern Man Pray?" *Newsweek*, 30 December 1968, pp. 38-39.

[3]"Evangelical Christianity in the United States: National Parallel Surveys of General Public and Clergy," conducted for *Christianity Today* by The Gallup Organization, Inc. and The Princeton Religion Research Center, 1979. A partial analysis of these surveys was published as "The Christianity Today-Gallup Poll: An Overview," *Christianity Today*, 21 December 1979, pp. 12-19.

[4]*Los Angeles Times*, 19 December 1984.

[5]The book I recommend more than any other is O. Hallesby, *Prayer* (Minneapolis: Augsburg, 1931). A list of "classics" would have to include books by E. M. Bounds, A. Murray, J. C. Ryle, R. A. Torrey and A. W. Tozer. The notes at the end of the book contain full references to many other helpful volumes. I've been especially helped by James I. Packer, *Knowing God* (Downers Grove, Ill.: InterVarsity Press, 1973); J. O. Sanders, *Prayer Power Unlimited* (Chicago: Moody Press, 1977); C. Murphey, *Prayerobics* (Waco, Tex.: Word, 1979); and J. G. S. S. Thompson, *The Praying Christ* (Grand Rapids, Mich.: Eerdmans, 1959). The last three are listed as out of print as I write this, but the books are worth going to a library to get.

[6]Donald G. Bloesch, *The Struggle of Prayer* (New York: Harper and Row, 1980), p. 11.

[7]See Matthew 5:19; 18:4; 20:26; 23:11.

[8]*The Four Loves* (London: Geoffrey Bles, 1960), p. 112.

Chapter 2: Holy

[1]*Ichthus* is a Greek word for "fish." Long before its ubiquitous use in jewelry, bumper stickers and wall plaques, this word and simple line drawings of fish were used in times of persecution to summarize the basis of Christian hope. It is an acrostic symbol representing the first letters of the Greek words for "Jesus Christ Son of God, [our] Savior."

²Robert E. Morosco, "Theological Implications of Fear," in H. Newton Malony, ed., *Wholeness and Holiness: Readings in the Psychology/Theology of Mental Health* (Grand Rapids, Mich.: Baker, 1983), pp. 122-23.

³Ibid., p. 127.

⁴Harry Blamires, *The Secularist Heresy: The Erosion of the Gospel in the Twentieth Century* (Grand Rapids, Mich.: Servant Books, 1980), pp. 13-14.

⁵It is unfortunate in this regard that many churches have dropped a time of confession of sin from their worship. It is doubtful that what a congregation's leadership elects to downplay in corporate spirituality will receive priority in members' prayer lives. The importance of confession in prayer and worship is helpfully emphasized in several recent books: R. W. Bailey, *New Ways in Christian Worship* (Nashville: Broadman Press, 1981); J. MacArthur, Jr., *The Ultimate Priority* (Chicago: Moody Press, 1983); R. G. Rayburn, *O Come, Let Us Worship* (Grand Rapids, Mich.: Baker, 1980); and R. E. Webber, *Worship: Old and New* (Grand Rapids, Mich.: Zondervan, 1982).

⁶John Owen, "Of the Mortification of Sin in Believers," in *The Works of John Owen*, vol. 4, ed. W. H. Goold (Philadelphia: Protestant Episcopal Book Society, 1862), p. 58.

⁷Hyssop was a bushy herb. Its branches were used in certain Jewish ritual purifications. See Leviticus 14:1-6 for an example. At the conclusion of the ceremony the priest was instructed to "pronounce him clean." Hyssop is mentioned twice in the New Testament: John 19:29 (in association with the death of Christ) and Hebrews 9:19 (with reference to the application of the "blood of the covenant" which Moses sprinkled on Israel). Some see an allusion to New Covenant forgiveness in David's light in light of the context given hyssop in Hebrews 9.

⁸See Matthew 5:4, 8. J. R. W. Stott, *The Message of the Sermon on the Mount* (Downers Grove, Ill.: InterVarsity Press, 1978), pp. 40-42, 48-49, is especially helpful: "Only the pure in heart will see God, see him now with the eye of faith and see his glory in the hereafter, . . . by whose fire all shams are burned up."

⁹Consider Hebrews 12:14 ("Without holiness no one will see the Lord") and James 4:8-10 ("Come near to God and he will come near to you. [How is this done?] Wash your hands, you sinners, and purify your hearts, you double-minded. Grieve, mourn and wail. Change your laughter to mourning and your joy to gloom. Humble yourselves before the Lord, and he will lift you up").

¹⁰Some may feel that this chapter gives the impression that personal holiness is a self-motivated endeavor. This, of course, is not the case. Holiness can never be a "do-it-yourself" program of moral striving accomplished solely on the strength of our unaided wills. Honest evaluation of such a self-effort program is expressed by Paul in Romans 7:24: "What a wretched man I am!" It is Christ, through his death and the gift of his Spirit, who makes it possible for believers to pursue holiness. The balance between our effort and the Spirit is nowhere more plain than in Philippians 2:12-13: "Continue to work out your salvation with fear and trembling, for it is God who works in you to will and to act according to his good purpose." This chapter focuses more on the first clause, the chapter on praying in Jesus' name gives more space to the work of Christ and the Spirit.

Chapter 3: All-Knowing
[1]Corpus Hermeticum 12. 18.
[2]Christian Science is probably the best-known modern form of gnosticism. See
Mary Baker Eddy's *Science and Health with Key to Scriptures* (Boston: First Church of
Christ Scientist, n.d.).
[3]Scripture is logical, often ruthlessly so. But Eastern thinkers have no difficulty
keeping in balance ideas which seem mutually exclusive to us in the West: "work
out your own salvation . . . for God is at work in you, both to will and to work
for his good pleasure" (Phil 2:12-13, RSV).
[4]See also Luke 21:17-18: "you will be hated by all on account of My name. Yet not
a hair on your head will perish" (NASB).

Chapter 4: Sovereign
[1]In the situation sketched, I've suggested that God's "response" must take place
before the prayer is offered. Such an idea presents a problem unless you remember
that God's existence is eternal, bound by neither space nor time. With God "a day
is like a thousand years" and conversely, "a thousand years are like a day" (2 Pet
3:8; Ps 90:4). God's "timelessness" has led theologians to speak of him as living in
an "eternal now." In the case of our birthday petition: the previous month's weather, today's prayer and next week's party would all be going on simultaneously for
God. To work in the future, God does not have to go back and adjust the past.
He acts in eternity, where everything that happens chronologically in the universe's space/time history always "is." For help in understanding this idea see K.
Boa, "Time," in *God, I Don't Understand* (Wheaton, Ill.: Victor Books, 1975), p. 90; C.
S. Lewis, "On Special Providences," in *Miracles: A Preliminary Study* (New York:
Macmillan, 1947), p. 187; and C. S. Lewis, "Time and Beyond Time," *Mere Christianity*, rev. ed. (London: Geoffrey Bles, 1952), pp. 134-35.
[2]J. I. Packer, "Providence," *The New Bible Dictionary*, 2nd ed. (Wheaton, Ill.: Tyndale,
1982), p. 990.
[3]Packer's statement, quoted above, contains the following Bible references which
I removed to make the text more readable: Ps 145:9; cf. Mt 5:45-48; Acts 17:28;
Col 1:17; Heb 1:3; cf. Ps 107; Job 1:12; 2:6; Gen 45:5-8; cf. Eph 1:9-12. There are
many more texts which might be given. Packer goes on to say that the biblical
conception of Providence, *i.e.*, God's relationship to the world as defined in the
quotation cited in note 1 above, distinguishes the scriptural point of view from:
　　(a) *pantheism*, which absorbs the world into God; (b) *deism*, which cuts it [the world]
　　off from him; (c) *dualism*, which divides control of it between God and another
　　power; (d) *indeterminism*, which holds that it is under no control at all; (e) *determi-
　　nism*, which posits a control of a kind that destroys man's moral responsibility;
　　(f) the doctrine of *chance*, which denies the controlling power to be rational; and
　　(g) the doctrine of *fate*, which denies it to be benevolent. (Ibid.).
Thoughtful reflection on these distinctions will suggest to some readers that, as
I think likely, some Christians actually hold deistic, dualistic, deterministic or fa-
talistic views about how God governs the world. Those holding these points of
view will find this chapter very hard to digest.

⁴Carl F. H. Henry, *God, Revelation and Authority*, vol. 5, *The God Who Stands and Stays* (Waco, Tex.: Word Books, 1982), pp. 303-4.

⁵Donald Bloesch, *Essentials of Evangelical Theology*, vol. 1, *God, Authority and Salvation* (San Francisco: Harper & Row, 1978), p. 28.

⁶See also L. Berkhof, *Systematic Theology* (Grand Rapids, Mich.: Eerdmans, 1946), p. 59; and Charles Hodge, *Systematic Theology*, vol. 1 (New York: Charles Scribner's Sons, 1885), p. 391.

⁷Alan Cole, *Exodus: An Introduction and Commentary*, Tyndale Old Testament Commentary Series (Downers Grove, Ill.: InterVarsity Press, 1973), p. 217.

⁸"The Christian is not to ask whether this or that event happened because of prayer. He is rather to believe that all events without exception are *answers* to prayer in the sense that whether they are grantings or refusals the prayers of all concerned and their needs have been taken into account. . . . There is no question *whether* an event has happened because of your prayer. When the event you prayed for occurs your prayer has always contributed to it. When the opposite event occurs your prayer has never been ignored; it has been considered and refused, for your ultimate good and the good of the whole universe. (For example, because it is better for you and for everyone else in the long run that other people, including wicked ones, should exercise free will than that you should be protected from cruelty or treachery by turning the human race into automata.)" Lewis, "On Special Providences," p. 187, italics his.

⁹S. D. Gordon, *Quiet Talks on Prayer* (1904; reprint ed., New York: Fleming Revell, 1980), p. 54.

¹⁰Ibid., p. 195.

¹¹When was the last time you were told that God has blessings all wrapped with a bow and your name on the tag and you could have them if you'd only pray for them? His dependency on your prayers is usually couched differently: He's a gentleman, and won't force himself—or his gifts—on anyone who doesn't ask (through prayer) for them. The text usually cited to support this is James 4:2: "You do not have because you do not ask" (NASB). However, in context this verse is explained by the following verse: Asking with "wrong motives" (lust and envy) is out of God's will and hence is no request at all.

¹²This is, of course, consistent with the definition of prayer given earlier in this book: Prayer is a means God uses to give us what he wants. Priority is placed on God's will. The tail does not wag the dog.

¹³C. S. Lewis, "The Efficacy of Prayer," in *The World's Last Night and Other Essays* (New York: Harcourt, Brace & Co., 1960), pp. 8-9. The essay first appeared in *The Atlantic Monthly*, January 1959.

¹⁴Packer, "Providence," p. 991.

¹⁵T. C. Hammond, "Can Prayer Change God's Mind?" *HIS* (November 1948), p. 4.

¹⁶Ibid., p. 5.

¹⁷"Some Pray and Die," *HIS* (August 1944), pp. 20-22. Christians are given a "break" of sorts in prayer because they have the Scriptures and the Holy Spirit to help them. Yet even the most saintly of people do not get all their prayers answered as they wish (2 Cor 12:8-9). Redemption does not make us omniscient.

[18]C. S. Lewis, *Miracles* (New York: Macmillan, 1944), p. 187.

Chapter 5: Spirit
[1]The word Jesus uses to express the idea that self-serving acts of "piety" make *no* impression on God ("no reward" in 6:1) is repeated three times: 6:2, 5 and 16. This term *apechousin* virtually means "paid in full and given a receipt—account closed." See W. Barclay, *A New Testament Wordbook* (London: SCM Press, 1955), pp. 17-20.

[2]See F. M. Cosgrove, Jr., "How to spend Personal Time with God," in *Essentials of New Life* (Colorado Springs: Navpress, 1978), pp. 79-95; and *Quiet Time: A Guidebook for Daily Devotions* (Downers Grove, Ill.: InterVarsity Press, 1976).

[3]This is what made it possible for Jesus to pray as he did in the garden of Gethsemane. "It was not the despairing cry for help of a man unaccustomed to prayer reduced to clutching at any straw. It was rather the action of one who had always found strength in prayer now desperately searching for the same strength through the usual channel." J. D. G. Dunn, *Jesus and the Spirit* (London: SCM Press, 1975), p. 20.

[4]See J. Jeremias, *The Prayers of Jesus* (Philadelphia: Fortress, 1978), p. 79.

[5]For an analysis of Luther's private prayer experiences see Walter Trobisch, *Martin Luther's Quiet Time* (Downers Grove, Ill.: InterVarsity Press, 1975).

[6]See especially A. W. Blackwood, *Leading in Public Prayer* (Grand Rapids, Mich.: Baker, 1975).

[7]There is a growing appreciation in evangelical Protestantism for time with God in which nothing is said. Contemplation and meditation on God and his Word are extremely important to many Christians. See J. Dowling, *Meditation: The Bible Tells You How* (Colorado Springs: Navpress, 1976); and Richard J. Foster, *Meditative Prayer* (Downers Grove, Ill.: InterVarsity Press, 1983).

Chapter 6: Good
[1]Arthur C. Custance, *The Silences of God* (Brookville, Ontario: Doorway Papers, 1971), pp. iii-iv.

[2]Robert Anderson, *The Silence of God* (London: Hodder and Stoughton, 1897), pp. 2, 7.

[3]I think it is precisely at such points when the intercession of the Holy Spirit on our behalf becomes especially important: "the Spirit himself intercedes for us with groans that words cannot express" (Rom 8:26; cf. 8:34); so also, of course, our willingness to "carry each other's burdens" (Gal 6:2) in intercessory prayer.

[4]Theodore Plantinga, *Learning to Live with Evil* (Grand Rapids, Mich.: Eerdmans, 1982).

[5]Alvera Mickelsen, "Why Did God Let It Happen?" *Christianity Today*, 16 March 1984, p. 23.

[6]That evil does *not* change into good from God's perspective seems plain from Romans 3:8. Those who say, "let us do evil that good may result," are justly condemned according to Paul. It is certainly obvious that God has and does work providentially in ways which result in so much good that the evil involved in a situation may *seem* appropriate to view in a positive way. Genesis 50:20, "you meant evil against me, but God meant it for good" (NASB, cf. 45:5, 7-8), might be cited

as such a case. But we must be very careful here. Joseph does not say his brothers' sin is now made into good—and he clearly implies that they remain accountable to God for the evil they intended: "Am I in God's place?" (50:19 NASB). Evil stays evil, even though God may bring some unforeseen good out of an evil circumstance. The amazing thing in Genesis 50 is Joseph's *lack of bitterness* toward God and his brothers. Like Jesus, "he learned obedience from what he suffered" and became "perfect" or complete, fully matured, in his faith in "the one who could save him from death" (Heb 5:7-8).

[7]In Revelation 6:9 those who have been slain by evil (and hence are with God) are not saying, "Now we understand," but "How long, Sovereign Lord, holy and true, until you judge . . . and avenge our blood?" Even in the presence of God himself, questions remain.

[8]Chuck Swindoll, *Encourage Me: Caring Words for Heavy Hearts* (Portland, Oreg.: Multnomah, 1982), pp. 43-44.

[9]Quoted ibid.

[10]Does God enjoy suffering and evil (cf. Ezek 18:22, 32)? Did Jesus lack "victorious faith" when he "offered up prayers and petitions with loud cries and tears" (Heb 5:7)?

[11]E. S. Gerstenberger and W. Schrage, *Suffering,* trans. H. E. Stelly (Nashville: Abingdon, 1980), p. 271.

The authors rightly say on the same page: "Prayer . . . puts us in the place where man in the last analysis, unable to discern God's governance, stands before him with empty hands and waits."

[12]Joseph Bayly, *The Psalms of My Life* (Wheaton, Ill.: Tyndale House, 1969). Text as printed is in Swindoll, *Encourage Me,* p. 13.

[13]Philip Yancey, *Where Is God When It Hurts?* (Grand Rapids, Mich.: Zondervan, 1978).

[14]Hugh Silvester, *Arguing with God: A Christian Examination of the Problem of Evil* (Downers Grove, Ill.: InterVarsity Press, 1971), pp. 124-25.

[15]A most helpful publication on this topic is C. Ohlrich, *The Suffering God: Hope & Comfort for Those Who Hurt* (Downers Grove, Ill.: InterVarsity Press, 1982).

Chapter 7: Father

[1]Sayings to this effect are preserved in the Babylonian Talmud: Berakoth 40a and Sanhedriyn 70b.

[2]See O. Hofius, "Father," in *The New International Dictionary of New Testament Theology,* ed. C. Brown, vol. 1 (Grand Rapids, Mich.: Zondervan, 1975), pp. 614-21.

[3]Jeremias, *Prayers of Jesus;* W. Marchel, *Abba Pere! Le prière du Christ et des chréteins,* (Rome: Biblical Institute Press, 1963).

[4]From the cross Jesus prays, "My God, My God," but this is a quotation of Psalm 22:1 and is the only exception.

[5]See on this J. E. Rosscup, *Abiding in Christ* (Grand Rapids, Mich.: Zondervan, 1973), especially "Abiding—with or without Effort," pp. 147-70.

[6]*Conditioned* can carry the notion that a person is brainwashed or externally coerced. A child repeatedly hit in the face by his father may be conditioned to flinch whenever the father raises his hand. I am *not* using the term above in this negative sense.

We can internalize positive ways of thinking (and behavior) through positive learning experiences. And this is the kind of learning, or conditioning, I refer to. Proverbs 22:6 is an Old Testament example; Romans 12:1-2 assumes it in the New Testament.

⁷The relationship between obedience to God's Word and prayer offered according to God's will is more complicated than the illustration in the text suggests. A fuller presentation of the process is diagrammed below.

The Prayer-Obedience Relationship

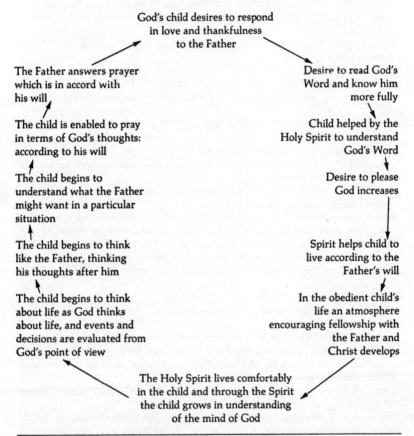

God's child desires to respond
in love and thankfulness
to the Father

The Father answers prayer
which is in accord with
his will

Desire to read God's
Word and know him
more fully

The child is enabled to pray
in terms of God's thoughts:
according to his will

Child helped by the
Holy Spirit to understand
God's Word

The child begins to
understand what the Father
might want in a particular
situation

Desire to please
God increases

The child begins to think
like the Father, thinking
his thoughts after him

Spirit helps child to
live according to the
Father's will

The child begins to think
about life as God thinks
about life, and events and
decisions are evaluated from
God's point of view

In the obedient child's
life an atmosphere
encouraging fellowship with
the Father and
Christ develops

The Holy Spirit lives comfortably
in the child and through the Spirit
the child grows in understanding
of the mind of God

"I urge you, brothers, in view of God's mercy, to offer your bodies as living sacrifices, holy and pleasing to God—which is your spiritual worship. Do not conform any longer to the pattern of this world, but be transformed by the renewing of your mind. *Then* you will be able to test and approve what God's will is—his good, pleasing and perfect will." (Rom 12:1-2)

Chapter 8: Thanking

¹If you struggle with this idea, you will find it helpful to read: Joan L. Guest, *Self-Esteem* (Downers Grove, Ill.: InterVarsity Press, 1984); B. Narramore, *You're Somebody Special* (Grand Rapids, Mich.: Zondervan, 1978); Blaine Smith, *One of a Kind* (Downers Grove, Ill.: InterVarsity Press, 1984); M. Wagner, *The Sensation of Being Somebody* (Grand Rapids, Mich.: Zondervan, 1976); or D. Wulf, *Find Yourself, Give Yourself: How Godly Self-respect Can Set You Free to Serve* (Colorado Springs: NavPress, 1983). See also these articles: D. Denk, " 'I Wanna Hold My Hand': Can We Love Ourselves Too Much?" *HIS*, March 1982, pp. 28-30; and J. R. W. Stott, "Am I Supposed to Love Myself or Hate Myself?" *Christianity Today*, 20 April 1984, pp. 26-28. All these authors draw a distinction between a healthy concept of ourselves in God's eyes and the godless "selfism" of modern pop psychology. For a helpful critique of selfism see Paul Vitz, *Psychology as Religion: The Cult of Self-Worship* (Grand Rapids, Mich.: Eerdmans, 1977).

²Tosephta Berakoth 4:1; Babylonian Berakoth 35a.

Chapter 9: Responding

¹God causes or permits many things in a believer's life, but too often God gets the blame for incidents which are caused by our inexperience, poor planning, ignorance, negligence, stupidity and animosity. Sure, God "causes" gravity, but if I drop an anvil on your toe, I, not God, am responsible.

²Laws of nature are empirically derived conclusions about how nature usually functions. Since God both created and sustains nature, the laws describe, but do not cause or control, what he has determined should normally occur for the functioning of the universe. God's actions, obviously, are *not* limited by what the laws of nature describe.

³J. B. Phillips, *Letters to Young Churches* (London: Fontana Books, 1955), pp. 13-14.

⁴C. S. Lewis, *The Problem of Pain* (New York: Macmillan, 1940), pp. 80-81.

⁵You may feel that character development is not a goal in God's discipline of unbelievers: that he only punishes them, or chastises them to lead them to repentance and faith. I agree that the latter is clearly God's major concern, but go on to note that Paul, for example, learned spiritually valuable lessons through discipline before his conversion ("It is hard for you to kick against the goads"), and that even militant atheists such as Bertrand Russell, for example, do become more compassionate through suffering. This could be called psychological conditioning or the like, but since Hebrews 12:8 says "everyone undergoes discipline," I view it as an aspect of God's so-called common grace given to all men and women.

⁶Though many Christians seem uncomfortable with the distinction I've drawn above between punishment and discipline, the differences were pointed out long ago by A. Strong. Strong's *Systematic Theology* asserts that "punishment is *essentially* different from chastisement [because] the latter proceeds from love [while punishment] proceeds *not* from love but from justice" (Old Tappan, N.J.: Revell,

1907), p. 653, emphasis mine.
[7]Lewis, *Problem of Pain*, pp. 34-36.

Chapter 10: Loving
[1]On the *agape* feast see W. Barclay, *The Letters to the Corinthians*, rev. ed. (Philadelphia: Westminster Press, 1975), pp. 100-102; W. Günther & H. Link, "Love," *New International Dictionary of New Testament Theology*, ed. Brown, 2:547; R. P. Martin, *Worship in the Early Church*, rev. ed. (Grand Rapids, Mich.: Eerdmans, 1974), pp. 120-29, 138-40; and Webber, *Worship: Old and New*, pp. 45-50.
[2]By this rendering the Amplified Bible expresses something of the force of the verb originally used by Peter. The word usually translated "hinder" (Greek: *enkoptesthai*) literally means "cut into or cut off."
[3]C. S. Lewis: *A Mind Awake*, ed. C. S. Kilby (London: Geoffrey Bles, 1968), p. 150.

Chapter 11: Forgiving
[1]See especially, Basilea Schlink, *Repentance: The Joy-filled Life*, trans. H. Corbin with S. Langer (Grand Rapids, Mich.: Zondervan, 1968).
[2]C. E. B. Cranfield, *A Critical and Exegetical Commentary on the Epistle to the Romans* (Edinburgh: T. & T. Clark, 1975), 2:649. For a full discussion see W. Klassen, "Coals of Fire: Sign of Repentance or Revenge?" *New Testament Studies* 9 (1962-63): 337-50.
[3]An example of such an excommunication is found in 1 Corinthians 5. 2 Corinthians 2:5-11 probably indicates that the guilty party repented and was forgiven and restored to the church with Paul's approval.
[4]An especially helpful book on this issue is J. White and K. Blue, *Healing the Wounded: The Costly Love of Church Discipline* (Downers Grove, Ill.: InterVarsity Press, 1985).
[5]On binding and loosing, see D. Hill, *The Gospel of Matthew* (Grand Rapids, Mich.: Eerdmans, 1972), pp. 258-64; and W. von Meding and D. Müller, "Bind," *New International Dictionary of New Testament Theology*, ed. Brown, 1:171-72.
[6]The reason an unforgiving spirit hinders prayer is found in Ephesians 4:30-31. Bitterness, anger and malice *grieve* the Holy Spirit, whose role it is to lead us into truth. Estranged from our Guide, we often wander into selfishness.

Chapter 12: Believing
[1]Quintus Septimius Florens Tertullianus (A.D. 160-215), an early Christian moralist and theologian, makes the statement in his *On The Body of Christ*, part 5: "It is to be believed absolutely, because it is absurd; . . . it is certain, because it is impossible."
[2]Lewis Carroll, *Through the Looking Glass* in *The Annotated Alice* (New York: Clarkson H. Potter, 1960), p. 251.
[3]Some assert on the basis of the grammar of Ephesians 2:8 that "Grace is God's part, faith ours." See A. T. Robertson, *Word Pictures in the New Testament*, vol. 4 (New York: Harper, 1931), p. 525. But J. R. W. Stott rightly says, "We must never think of salvation as a kind of transaction between God and us in which he contributes grace and we contribute faith. For we were dead, and had to be quickened before we could believe" (*The Message of Ephesians* [Downers Grove, Ill.: InterVarsity Press,

1979], p. 83). "*It* is the gift of God" and "*this* is not of yourself" refer to the whole preceeding clause, "by grace you have been saved, through faith," and to everything connected with salvation. See A. S. Wood, "Romans," *The Expositor's Bible Commentary,* ed. F. E. Gaebelein (Grand Rapids, Mich.: Zondervan, 1978), 11:36; and W. Hendriksen, *Ephesians* (Grand Rapids, Mich.: Baker, 1967), pp. 120-23. That faith is a gift is plainly taught in Acts 18:27 and Philippians 1:29. This notion does not hang on Ephesians 2:8 alone; indeed it could not because the grammar is not precise enough.

[4]B. F. Westcott, *The Epistle to the Hebrews,* 2nd ed. (London: Macmillan, 1892), p. 127.

[5]This is the central point in A. Prator's *How Much Faith Does It Take?* (Nashville: Thomas Nelson, 1982). For more rigorous discussions see R. Dunn, *The Faith Crisis: What faith is, what it isn't, and why it doesn't always do what we want it to do* (Wheaton, Ill.: Tyndale House, 1984); and W. R. Spear, *The Theology of Prayer* (Grand Rapids, Mich.: Baker, 1979), esp. pp. 50-58.

[6]If some of the names on this list seem strange you might enjoy investing some of your leisure reading J. D. Douglas, ed., *The New International Dictionary of the Christian Church,* 2nd ed. (Grand Rapids, Mich.: Zondervan, 1979). The articles are fascinating, well written and short enough to take the book up and put it down as time is available. Bibliographies are provided so you can ask your librarian or bookstore for a full biography on persons you'd like to learn more about. Visit your church library: look under "Biography." Chances are there's some super stuff—genuine spiritual encouragement, just waiting there to be discovered.

[7]Müller's own words are: "It is true that the faith, which I am enabled to exercise, is altogether God's own gift; it is true that He alone supports it, and that He alone can increase it; it is true that, moment by moment, I depend upon Him for it, and that, if I were only one moment left to myself, my faith would utterly fail; but it is not true that my faith is that gift of faith which is spoken of in I Corinthians 12:9 . . . it is the self-same faith which is found in every believer. . . ." R. Steer, *George Müller: Delighted in God* (Wheaton, Ill.: Harold Shaw, 1975), pp. 76-77. This volume is the best of the Müller biographies and the picture of Müller which emerges from Steer's research is to be preferred over most others.

[8]A. Rendle Short, ed., *The Diary of George Müller* (Grand Rapids, Mich.: Zondervan, 1972), p. 72, emphasis mine.

Chapter 13: Persisting

[1]C. S. Lewis, "Religion: Reality or Substitute?" in *Christian Reflections,* ed. W. Hooper (Grand Rapids, Mich.: Eerdmans, 1967), p. 43.

[2]"In the course of time the deeper meaning of fasting, as an expression of man's humbling of himself before God, was lost for Israel. Increasingly it came to be [wrongly] regarded as a pious achievement. The struggle of the prophets against this depersonalization and emptying of the concept (cf. Isa. 58:3-7; Jer. 14:12) was without success." F. S. Rothenberg, "Fasting," *New International Dictionary of New Testament Theology,* ed. Brown, 1:612. Even after Jesus' teaching, fasting is still misunderstood.

[3]C. E. B. Cranfield, *The Gospel According to St. Mark* (Cambridge: At the University

Press, 1966), p. 186. The story is more poignant than it seems. Such an illness would have rendered a Jewish woman ceremonially unclean and thus prevented her from access to God through the Temple. Jesus also gave her fellowship with God, something *go in peace* may imply, for which she must have been extremely thankful.

[4]The words *and fasting* are added in some Greek manuscripts. They are omitted in recent translations undertaken by Bible-believing scholars such as the *New American Standard Bible* and the *New International Version*. For scholarly analysis, see Cranfield, *St. Mark*, pp. 304-5.

[5]"It would be healthier if all Christians were as honest as Asaph instead of pretending that they always walk in the full light of Christ." H. L. Ellison, *The Psalms* (London: Scripture Union, 1967), p. 66.

Chapter 14: Christ: Our Example

[1]References to all of Jesus' prayers are given in the appendix at the back of the book.
[2]Those who do not know God as Father are invited to approach him through Christ. On the basis of the historical reality of God's creatorship, our sinfulness and Christ's death on the cross and resurrection, God invites and commands us now to:

A. *Turn* from our rebellion to Christ as Lord with our whole selves in our
1. *Minds:* Agree with God that we have wronged him and deserve his judgment.
2. *Emotions:* Despise our sins and our sinful nature.
3. *Wills:* Determine to turn from our rebellion and serve our Creator and Redeemer. See Christ as the payer for, and the power over, our sin.
Bible texts which support this are Is 55:7; 12:1-3; 1 Thess 1:9-10.
B. *Trust* in nothing that we can do, but only in the finished work of Christ as Savior with our
1. *Minds:* Recognize Christ as the necessary and sufficient payment for sin.
2. *Emotions:* Long for Christ and rejoice in his love for the undeserving.
3. *Wills:* Commit our lives to Christ by casting ourselves upon him as our only hope for reconciliation with God. Transfer our trust from ourselves to him. Take for ourselves his gift of forgiveness and righteousness. Ask for God's mercy.
Bible texts which support this are Jn 1:12; Rom 3:21-26; Jn 3:16.
A person can only become a Christian—a child of God by faith—by turning from a sinful life to Christ and by trusting him as Savior and Lord. There is a cost to becoming a disciple of Jesus. Read Mark 8:34-38 and Luke 14:25-33.
This biblical approach is taken from W. Metzger, *Tell the Truth: The Whole Gospel to the Whole Person by Whole People* (Downers Grove, Ill.: InterVarsity Press, 1981) p. 47.
[3]Did he, for example, pray on his bed as David (Ps 4:4) or sitting down under a tree as Elijah (1 Kings 19:4)? Did he lift up his hands when he looked up to heaven as suggested by Psalm 134:2 and prescribed by Paul in 1 Timothy 2:8?

Chapter 15: Concluding

[1]The similar expression, *through Jesus Christ,* is only used three times (Rom 1:8; 7:25;

16:27). All the New Testament prayers are listed at the end of the book so you can examine the evidence for yourself.

²In the second and third centuries such formulae were often used in the liturgical prayers which came to characterize Christian worship.

³The notion that *in my name* equals spiritual leverage or some form ot clout is completely debunked by these verses. Is Jesus likely to be impressed with the authority of his own name? Further, such views fly in the face of the evidence. "It is not inappropriate, due to the economy of redemption, to speak of the Son acting on the authority of the Father (cf. Jn 8:42), but *nowhere* does the Scripture speak of the Father acting on the authority of the Son." Spear, *Theology of Prayer*, p. 33, emphasis mine.

⁴So also, RV, RSV and JB. The NEB and NIV—*against* the Greek word order— harmonize the verse with 16:24 and 26, rendering: "my Father will give you whatever you ask in my name." This is not the place to argue about translational philosophy, but it is notable that NEB and NIV *do* follow carefully the Greek word order in rendering 16:24 and 26. No one knows whether the change in word order is merely stylistic (which NIV and NEB seem to assume). If not—as I think likely— it is unfortunate the difference (from "asking" to "giving" in Jesus' name) has been obscured in the NIV and NEB. (Compare Psalm 24:11 where the psalmist petitions God in his name.)

⁵For a comprehensive discussion, see J. E. Rosscup, *Abiding in Christ* (Grand Rapids, Mich.: Zondervan, 1973).

⁶F. F. Bruce, *The Gospel of John* (Grand Rapids, Mich.: Eerdmans, 1983), p. 309, emphasis mine. Bruce goes on to make the important observation that "Jesus himself is the living embodiment of all his teaching."

⁷J. R. W. Stott, *Christ the Liberator* (Downers Grove, Ill.: InterVarsity Press, 1971), p. 57, emphasis mine.

⁸The NIV rendering "Then" at the beginning of the second sentence expresses this clearly. There is a similar conditionality suggested by the use of "if" in John 15:7 and 10. The same thing is seen in Romans 12:2, "Do not conform any longer to the pattern of this world, but be transformed by the renewing of your mind. *Then* you will be able to test and approve what God's will is."

⁹Thus, although we have focused on it above, the believer's obedience is not to be viewed as meritorious. It does not earn us a hearing. As shown in chapter 7 it *demonstrates* that we love the Father and the Savior, it *distinguishes* the child of God from the rebellious world, and it is used by the Holy Spirit to *train* us to pray according to God's will.

¹⁰Judaism also used the expression *name of the Lord* as a way of avoiding saying God's covenant name. It was thought that this would help prevent any misuse of God's name in violation of Exodus 20:7.

¹¹Many scholars write about the significance of names in Scripture. See for example, J. A. Motyer, "Name," *New Bible Dictionary*, pp. 810-13; W. K. Kaiser, Jr., "Name," *Zondervan Pictorial Encyclopedia of the Bible*, 5 vols. (Grand Rapids, Mich.: Zondervan, 1975), 4:360-66, esp. p. 363; or H. Bietenhard and F. F. Bruce, "Name," *New International Dictionary of New Testament Theology*, ed. Brown, 2·648-56.

[12]B. F. Westcott, *The Gospel According to St. John* (1881; reprint ed., Grand Rapids, Mich.: Zondervan, 1957), p. 204. See also W. Hendriksen, *The Gospel of John* (Grand Rapids, Mich.: Baker, 1954), p. 274: "a prayer in Christ's name is a prayer that is in harmony with whatever Christ has revealed about himself."

[13]S. Chadwick, *The Path of Prayer* (London: Marshall, Morgan and Scott, 1936), p. 53. So also R. E. Brown, *The Gospel According to John XII-XXI* (New York: Doubleday, 1970), p. 636: "A Christian prays in Jesus' name in the sense that he is in union with Jesus."

[14]These conclusions are based on a more detailed analysis by myself and others than is necessary or appropriate to present in a book like this. Unfortunately this work is so technical that it will be available only to those with access to a major biblical research library at a seminary or university: J. McPolin, *The "Name" of the Father and of the Son in the Johannine Writings* (Ph.D. diss., Rome: Pontifical Biblical Institute, 1971); F. G. Untergassmair, *Im Namen Jesu: Der Namesbegriff im Johannesevangelium* Forschung zur Bibel 13 (Stuttgart: Katholisches Bibelwerk, 1974; J. Caba, *La oración de petición,* Analecta Biblica 62 (Rome: Biblical Institute Press, 1974); W. Bingham Hunter, *The Prayers of Jesus in the Gospel of John* (Ph.D. diss., University of Aberdeen, 1979).

Appendix

[1]Herbert Lockyer, *All the Prayers of the Bible* (Grand Rapids, Mich.: Zondervan, 1959).

Index of Scripture References